Dottie Temple and Stan Finegold

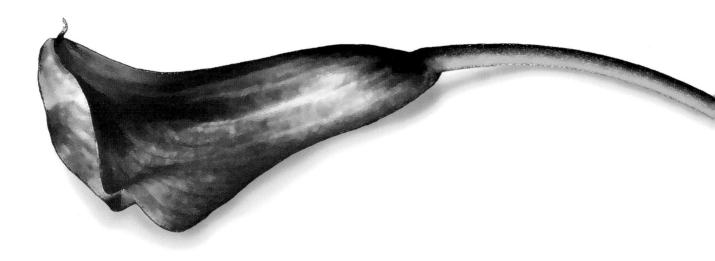

SENIOR WRITER
Leslie F. Cavalier

CONTEMPORARY PHOTOGRAPHY
Rob Cardillo

INTRODUCTION AND SIDEBARS
William Seale

FLOWERS

WHITE HOUSE STYLE

simon & schuster

NEW YORK LONDON TORONTO SYDNEY SINGAPORE

SIMON & SCHUSTER
Rockefeller Center
1230 Avenue of the Americas
New York, NY 10020

SIMON & SCHUSTER and colophon are registered
trademarks of Simon & Schuster, Inc.

A complete list of photo credits appears on page 209.

For information about special discounts for bulk purchases,
please contact Simon & Schuster Special Sales:
1-800-456-6798 or business@simonandschuster.com

Designed by Amy Hill

Manufactured in the United States of America

1   3   5   7   9   10   8   6   4   2

Library of Congress Cataloging-in-Publication Data
Temple, Dottie.
Flowers, White House style / Dottie Temple and Stan Finegold;
senior writer, Leslie F. Cavalier; contemporary photography, Rob Cardillo;
introduction and sidebars, William Seale.
p. cm
1. Floral decorations—United States. 2. Flower arrangement—United States.
3. White House (Washington, D.C.)—Anecdotes. I. Finegold, Stan. II. Title.
SB449.T42 2002
745.92'0973—dc21   2002075813

ISBN 0-7432-2334-9

To Chrissie and Diane for all their help in dragging me into the twenty-first-century world of computers and for their untiring effort in keeping me on the right track. To Phil, for allowing me to take precious time out of our lives to do this book. My love to you all, and thank you.

— *Dottie*

To my sage wife and partner, Leslie, who helps me every day to keep our hectic lives afloat with grace and humor, and to my daughter, Ariel, for being the most inspirational, rewarding, and beautiful part of my life.

— *Stan*

acknowledgments

First of all, I wish to thank the First Ladies who gave me the opportunity of working in the White House, Betty Ford, Rosalynn Carter, and especially Nancy Reagan, for giving me the chance, in my small way, to play a part in America's history. Secondly, I want to thank their most capable social secretaries: Muffie Cabot, Gahl Burt, Maria Downs, Nancy Ruwe, and Tish Baldrige. Most of all, however, I would like to thank Rex Scouten, the Chief Usher during my years at the White House. His calm demeanor and clear judgment in the most difficult circumstances inspired us all.

— *Dottie*

The creation of this book required the talent, patience, generosity, and effort of many people. We are indebted to these skillful archivists at the presidential libraries: David Stanhope and Polly Nodine at the Jimmy Carter Library, Nancy Mirshah at the Gerald R. Ford Library, Allan Goodrich at the John F. Kennedy Library, J. Philip Scott and Shannon Jarret at the Lyndon Baines Johnson Library, DeNeine Bradley and Sam McClure at the Nixon Presidential Materials of the National Archives and Record Administration, Olivia S. Anastasiadis and Susan Naulty at the Richard Nixon Birthplace, Mary Finch and Stephanie Oriabure at the George W. Bush Library, Steve Branch at the Ronald Reagan Library, Kevin Cartwright at the Nixon Library, Deborah Bush at the Clinton Presidential Materials, and Harmony Haskins at the White House Historical Association. We also greatly appreciate the assistance of Betty Monkman and Lydia Tederick in the Office of the Curator at the White House.

We are very grateful to Ann Sink; Betsy Gullan of the Pennsylvania Horticultural Society; Marilyn Whitmore, President of the Garden Club Federation of Pennsylvania; and Dorothy Nace of the Garden Club Federation of Bala Cynwyd for their support in helping us find beautiful homes in which to photograph Ms. Temple's contemporary floral arrangements, as well as to the gracious homeowners who opened their doors to us: Mr. and Mrs. George Q. Nichols; Bill and Ann Hozak and their daughter, Cathy; Oliver and Mary

Biddle, Sallie and Bert Korman, and Carrie Sullivan of Pohlig Builders for the use of its Harriton Farms Model Home. Special thanks to Tom Keane of Cut Flower Exchange of Pennsylvania for his cooperation in providing us with such gorgeous blooms for our arrangements. And our appreciation to Henry Haller and Bess Abel, whose interview about her years as social secretary to Lady Bird Johnson never ceases to delight us.

Thank you to Beatrice Finegold, Shirley Oppenheim, Jonathan Kremer, Professor Barbara Carson, Chris Leaman, and Mark and Judith Rifkin for their assistance during the development of the book's concept. Also, the contributions of several makers of fine decorative table items were invaluable in dressing many of our modern arrangement photographs: Michael Puleo of Mottahedah, Julia Stambules of Waterford Wedgwood, and Christina LeBaron of Steuben. Thanks also to the great people at Verdissimo for their wonderful freeze-dried material.

Our heartfelt thanks to our advisers and attorneys, Lloyd Remick and Amanda Gross, for their tireless enthusiasm for this project and all of our endeavors. We are also indebted to Diane Brodeur and Christina King for all of their superlative work and pleasant demeanor despite our demands.

We offer our deepest gratitude to the team of professionals who brought this idea of a White House floral history to life on these pages: to Rita Rosenkranz for loving the idea, helping us to refine the book concept, and giving it wings with the greatest publisher in the world; to Constance Herndon for believing in the concept; to our highly capable editor, Sydny Miner (and her assistant, Laura Holmes), for taking our collection of photographs, text, and arrangement instructions and creating a book of which we are immensely proud; to Amy Hill and Jonathon Brodman for meticulously finishing each page with great care; to William Seale for imparting his passion for history and the importance of flowers in the President's house; to Rob Cardillo (and his very able assistant, John Bansemer) for his generosity and unique sensitivity in capturing the beauty of Dottie Temple's arrangements; and to Leslie F. Cavalier, whose attention to detail, exceptional talent in the craft of writing, and wonderful skill in melding memoirs with research made this book possible.

— *Stan and Dottie*

contents

1

THE FLOWER SHOP AT
1600 PENNSYLVANIA AVENUE

2

GUIDELINES FOR GRAND DESIGN

3

FORMAL CONTAINERS AND VASES

4

INFORMAL AND WHIMSICAL CONTAINERS

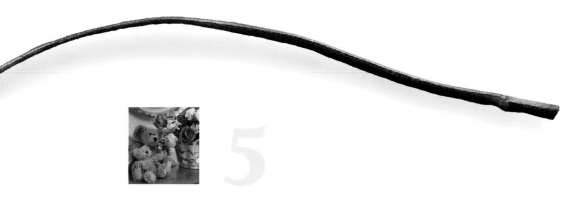

A NOTE FROM NANCY REAGAN

Flowers have always been very important to me—a room without them seems cold and uninviting. I particularly felt this when we moved into the White House. When we were there, I felt there should be flowers in every room, all the time. I think—and hope—it made the rooms much more inviting for all the tours that came through every day. Of course, I had the help of a lot of wonderful people to whom I'm very grateful.

— Nancy Reagan

Flowers, White House Style

introduction

WILLIAM SEALE

The inside workings of seats of power are an eternal fascination for those outside looking in. Indiscreet gossip by a royal chef gave the world some of what it knows about intimacies within the Roman villa of Caesar and Cleopatra; Napoleon's valet, Louis Constant, reported in three volumes the minutiae of the Emperor's private life, from how he staged his ceremonies to how he shaved his face to his customary mode of seduction. The house of the most powerful head of state in the world today attracts no less interest. This book opens up a very particular area of White House life, taking you into the crowded cellar florist studio beneath the lawn which produces the beautiful flower arrangements that surround the President of the United States and enhance the wonderful rooms of his house.

Flowers are held in high regard at the White House. When they are not there—which is very rare—they are sorely missed. They help bring tranquility to a frantically busy place where even the chimes of the clocks are silenced so as not to distract from the work of the day. In antique vases of bronze and porcelain, flowers of all kinds bring color and artistic design to the stately historical rooms. The floral arrangements are performances in themselves, expressive pieces with as many moods as can be had. On a marble mantel, massive arrangements of pink roses swim in the endless pools of reflection created by the tall mirrors that face each other across the East Room. In the center of the Blue Room a spring bouquet of tulips rivals the lofty, silky elegance of the space. Lesser rooms are also not neglected. And the family quarters are continually supplied with fresh flower arrangements; as one begins to wither, another takes its place.

That is not the end of it. The President frequently entertains, and special flower arrangements are required for these functions. This means bouquets for the state rooms and centerpieces for the dinner table or tables. It can mean several hundred arrangements for large dinners held beneath tents and canopies on the South Lawn. In the florist shop the flowers come and go. For large affairs, the arrangements are sometimes lined up in the open-air areaway on the north side of the house, awaiting placement inside. Telephone and computer orders fly out with botanical names for flowers of just a certain type and color. Delivery trucks thread Washington streets taking long boxes of flowers to the White House, always after scrutiny by the Secret Service.

In the early years of the White House, artificial flowers had been used in abundance. The earliest record of these describes the wax flowers President James Monroe used on the great thirteen-foot bronze-and-mirror plateau he had ordered from France for his banquet table. Flowers made of wax had the delicate subtle coloring and form of the real thing and enjoyed a long history of use in the state rooms of the White House. President Andrew Jackson, one of the great garden patrons among the presidents, had camellias in pots brought in from the greenhouse and stood about. Jessie Benton Fremont remembered their beautiful blossoms during entertainments at the White House.

Prior to the mid-nineteenth century, people had certain objections, however, to flowers inside the house. Very conscious of health, they believed flowers drank up oxygen in the air and sent harmful vapors into the room. But the interest in flower arranging with fresh flowers seems to have begun in the late 1840s and flourished in the 1850s. During the 1850s, dinner guests at the White House could expect a nosegay at a lady's plate and a boutonniere at a man's. Gold-lace paper framed the nosegays: stiff, symmetrical bouquets the size of a salad plate, usually made of roses. The greenhouse of the White House, founded in fact as an orangery by Andrew Jackson in 1834 to provide healthful winter citrus, yielded a bounty of camellias and sasanquas, which may often have found their way into both nosegays and boutonnieres. An occasional mention of violets varied the style, and summer garden flowers were always available in the White House garden. Toward the mid-1850s, geraniums became a mania among flower arrangers, appearing in nosegays at the White House, as well as in florist shops along Pennsylvania Avenue. The brittleness of their stems was not the problem one might have thought.

Fresh flower arrangements were introduced to the White House about 1857 by Harriet Lane, surrogate First Lady in the presidency of her uncle, the bachelor James Buchanan. A redhead in her twenties, she had served as his hostess in London, when he was American minister to the court of Queen Victoria. Her tutelage in that formal but royal circle showed in the elegant social manner she introduced at the White House. Remembering those antebellum days, people long afterward would contend that Buchanan's had been the most splendid White House of the entire nineteenth century.

Perhaps its grandeur was shaped in part by the drama of the times. The Civil War was imminent, and tensions between the North and the South were almost unbearable, even across White House dinner tables. As the four years of the administration passed, the President began to weed out and rearrange the guest lists in order to separate increasingly hostile political rivals. Of course, if they were elected officials he had to include them in his entertainments no matter how threatening they were, but he divided them up among different evenings, according to their views.

The White House of this period saw large arrangements everywhere. Harriet Lane purchased a circular sofa for the Blue Room, equipped with a central vase for flowers often associated with old-time hotel lobbies. By then Andrew Jackson's greenhouse had been rebuilt atop the West Wing of the house and could be easily reached from the hall of the state floor. In heavy terra-cotta pots placed on wooden tables, brightly colored single-petal roses flourished, along with pink and red camellias, palms, and the popular white lilies of the time. The flower arrangements were made presumably by the gardener, possibly the butler, or even Harriet Lane herself.

Here in 1858, President Buchanan's niece, Harriet Lane, walks in the new conservatory attached to the White House. She appreciated the camellias as well as the exotic South American orange trees, aloes, and pitcher plants. On visiting days, the public was permitted to enjoy the conservatory.

At a State Dinner on March 9, 1871, guests marveled at the Monroe plateau, elaborated with arches and orchids, Mrs. Julia Grant's favorite flower.

Abraham Lincoln continued the flower arrangements at the White House, just as he followed every other one of Buchanan's social customs to the letter. A visiting cousin remembered that Mrs. Lincoln took an interest in flower arranging and mistakenly attributed the custom's beginning at the White House to her. Lincoln's wife often wore fresh flowers in her hair, as well as artificial ones. To avoid getting bruised hands at public receptions, she carried a bouquet, making it impossible to shake hands with her. At Lincoln's funeral service in the East Room, some among the two thousand guests packed around the coffin were lulled and sickened by the heavy scent of the numerous spring flower arrangements and floral offerings.

But the real flower world of the White House did not get under way until the administration of Ulysses S. Grant. The great war hero's election marked a wish for the nation to return to harmony, and the Grants in the White House symbolized the ideal, successful American family. Julia Dent Grant understood the challenge perfectly. The entertainments were many.

Grant, an idolized celebrity as well as the President, was the star attraction, and Mrs. Grant saw to it that the jewel shimmered in the proper setting.

And thus flower arranging arose full force. Julia Grant's White House, as she described it, was "a world of orchids." As Andrew Jackson before her had encouraged the expansion of gardening in the grounds, Mrs. Grant created a world of flowers inside the house. She employed more gardeners and greenhouse specialists, people able to arrange flowers as well as tend them. The greenhouse was now called the "conservatory," and was expanded. Orchids were her favorites, and the greenhouse soon had an orchid room. Flowers massed in vases were found on tables and mantels, in windows, and on stands. Every detail interested the First Lady. She loathed the old mirrored Monroe plateau in the dining room. Trying to improve it, she added to it a conceit of copper screening that she had stuffed with blossoms, giving the effect of fanciful ribbons arching the old mirror base. This also did not entirely please her. Struggling with it unsuccessfully for most of her eight years in the White House, she finally sent the plateau to storage. What appeared in its place was a *pièce de résistance* she bought at the Centennial celebration of 1876 in Philadelphia: a silver statue of Hiawatha, paddling his canoe in a mirrored Gitchie-Goomie. This received her orchids and roses, smilax, baby's breath, palm leaves, and ferns very well.

When her White House days came to an end, Julia Grant, fighting back tears, nevertheless was game enough to hold a "pink luncheon" for the incoming Mrs. Hayes. She planned it in every particular, complete with a table massed with pink azaleas and something of a bower or cloud created over the chair to be occupied by the honoree, laden with more pink azaleas.

The silk train of the flamboyant Julia Grant had hardly swept over the White House floor for the last time when the saintly Lucy Webb Hayes entered, the darling of the temperance movement and also a great lover of flowers. Although she soon became famous for banning alcohol of all kinds from the White House, she is less well known for encouraging the gardeners. During Rutherford B. Hayes's one term, the number of garden and greenhouse staff increased to include five "bouquet makers" or flower arrangers. These were the first full-time flower arrangers in the White House.

The source of their importance was actually political. Since the beginning of the nineteenth century, in a custom begun by Dolley Madison, the First Lady had been expected to call upon any woman of importance who came to town. This meant every congressman's wife, every senator's, every major official's, important businessmen's, foreign minister's—and so on. It had been easy enough in the early days, when few wives actually came to Washington. But by the 1870s, railroad trains were unloading large numbers of important visitors who came to the capital as social guests and for business. Many congressmen and senators were joined in Washington by their wives. The prospect of calling on so many people was dizzying, not to say practically an impossibility. By the 1840s, first ladies were having the coachman deliver their cards sometimes instead of calling in person. This greatly diluted the honor that a personal visit had been.

Mrs. Grant's approach to the problem was to have bouquets made for the most important people and have the coachman deliver them. It met with success. Mrs. Hayes expanded the idea by sending out dozens of bouquets, sometimes in a single day, at first with her card and then with a specially printed card explaining that the bouquet was a gift from the President and First Lady and how to care for it. Gold and silver lace paper, ribbons, and all sorts of trimmings apparently made these presentations very handsome.

The bouquet makers stayed very busy, working under the direction of Henry Pfister, the head gardener hired by Hayes. They made two huge wedding bells from white roses for the Hayeses' twenty-fifth wedding anniversary celebration in the East Room. The house was decorated for the many, albeit "dry," dinners, luncheons, teas, and garden parties that came to characterize the rich, hospitable Hayeses.

The gardeners' work was only less intense during the brief Garfield administration, and, except perhaps for dinners, the widower President Chester A. Arthur seems to have been happy with a rose for his lapel.

However, they were called to labor harder than ever in 1886 for the marriage in the Blue Room of

President Grover Cleveland to the youthful Frances Folsom, at whose feet the American public fell worshipfully prostrate.

Mindful of the great difference in ages between bride and groom, the bouquet makers strained for symbolism. The hearth of the Blue Room blazed with salvia. Festoons of greenery and flowers swagged the walls, the gaslight was banked in ferns, and palms ringed the room. In the dining room the climax of the wedding decorations surmounted the table, a Temple of Hymen made from orchids and roses. The bride was fond of flowers. Now and then, in later days, she would stop in the greenhouse and admire a rose or orchid. If Pfister, the gardener, happened to see it, he would call up to Octavius Pruden, an artistic member of the office staff, who would hurry down and paint the blossom to present to her as a picture. Other times Pfister would pull the chosen flower and dispatch a chambermaid to pin it to her pillow.

The riot of Victorian flower arranging continued through the century's end, when ambassadors began to replace ministers in Washington—from the year 1898, when the nation emerged on the international scene, through the fall of 1901, when the bouquet makers draped the house in black for the assassinated William McKinley. They piled his coffin with flower arrangements formed into flags and presidential shields; they banked the walls with their creations, to be taken to the Capitol for the funeral and then on a train to Ohio.

The new president, Theodore Roosevelt, was to change things in the course of dramatizing the new presidency for which McKinley had set the stage. His first state dinner, held in honor of Prince Henry of Prussia, then traveling incognito in the United States, was too large for the dining room as it then was, so it was held in the East Room. The bouquet makers adorned the long, white-covered table with pink roses in tall glass vases that made umbrellalike spreads over the elegantly laid repast. Flower arranging was an interest of Mrs. Roosevelt. She liked rather more simple arrangements than had been White House fare for the past forty years or more.

The conservatories gave her great pleasure, and she was not unmindful of their political value. When her husband decided that it was time to transform the White House to make a better background for the new presidency, the architect Charles McKim declared that the rambling "glass houses" on the west side obstructed his best efforts and would have to be removed. Edith Roosevelt protested to her husband, and a standoff ensued. At last, during the summer of 1902, while the Roosevelts were relaxing at their home on Long Island, McKim finally got his way. He called his triumph the Treaty of Oyster Bay.

McKim's remodeled White House had a traditional look on the outside. But inside, the original house was nearly obscured by the smart international look he had created. The image inside was neoclassical and European, to fit a new world power. Dark English oak contrasted with polished white and gold; walls were covered with velvet, stone, and white plaster—the entire effect was new and formal by contrast. Indeed, some said it was regal, compared to what the White House had ever been. The conservatories were gone. So were the Victorian concepts of fancy floral pieces.

Floral art at the White House was now in harmony with the revised interiors. It included tall vases containing long-stemmed roses or rubrum lilies, tubs of clipped laurel or palms, mantel containers holding ivy and roses or seasonal flowers. Alice Roosevelt's wedding was very restrained, with jasmine and white orchids; Ethel Roosevelt's debut in 1908 featured small Christmas trees on round dinner tables set up in the new ground-floor rooms. Flowers in the twentieth-century White House were subdued compared to what had been. Greenery and flowers were now subtle accents to the architecture and decor. As the years passed, this style was used more and more. Except for a wedding or funeral, flower arrangements at the White House became relatively simple. The greenhouses, disassembled and rebuilt in different forms on the Mall, remained for many more years under Henry Pfister, but, no longer being connected to the White House, their use was more complicated. Florists' bills began to appear among the presidents' household papers.

No revival occurred for more than half a century. Stiff, domed "florist"-style arrangements became a household staple at the White House. While flowers still played a role, they were in evidence usually during receptions, dinners, or other occasions and their designs were very restrained. Roses topped the list of preferred flowers. Carnations followed—always white in the Red Room—and occasionally lilies, filling the historic vases that had been used for more than a hundred years. The great plateau was used full length by President Dwight D. Eisenhower around 1953. After that most of it was packed up, not to be assembled in its entirety again until the Clinton administration, more than forty years later. During the next decade, flowers in the White House were arranged by staff members or ordered from florists. They were burdens on the executive budget and used with restraint.

Not until the Kennedy administration, when so much about the White House was rethought and rephrased, did flowers again become a special interest of the President and his wife. In the organization and cataloging of White House furnishings, flower containers were made a special category. Cellar rooms and obscure closets were searched for vases, and the resulting collection proved to be excellent, with high points being the porcelain urns purchased for James Monroe in France in 1817 and the grand gold-plated containers that were part of the vermeil collection donated during the Eisenhower administration. Jacqueline Kennedy is remembered for liking a variety of floral arrangements, sometimes even using vegetables instead of flowers. Her enthusiasm for floral art reinvigorated the use of flowers at the White House. ✎

It is not known exactly when White House teas began, but by the end of the Hayes administration in 1881 they were a staple of entertaining. Here a lithograph of Mrs. Hayes' "Pink Tea" in the State Dining Room shows the room, food, and the house party decorated all in pink.

foreword

DOTTIE TEMPLE

Flowers have played an important role in my life since I was a very young child.

My grandparents' gardens were a strong focus in their lives, and my mother had the loveliest rock garden around. My fascination with flowers started almost as soon as I could walk, as I vividly remember picking dandelions and buttercups. My efforts were rewarded early on when, at the age of seven, my father started taking me along to visit a dear friend who raised carnations in his greenhouse.

On each visit I was allowed to help myself to the not-so-perfect blossoms. These "rescue" trips offered me endless hours of fun making bouquets for my family and friends. May Day was a favorite holiday of mine. I would decorate baskets with bits of crepe paper and fill them with wild and tended flowers that I would then secretly hang on neighbors' doors.

What a charming practice—maybe it's time for a revival. After high school, I attended Norfolk County Agricultural School, in Massachusetts, and planned a career in landscape architecture. At that time women were rare in this field; I was the only female in the entire school.

Among the requirements for a diploma was glazing a greenhouse. This was accomplished by climbing a ladder up the side of the house, removing a leaky pane of glass, cleaning the frame, replacing the glass, and recaulking it. As it happens, I'm afraid of heights, and in my fright I knocked the ladder over and my foot went through a perfectly sound pane of glass on the side of the greenhouse. My instructor was not the least bit understanding and graded me accordingly. My next disappointment was learning to drive a tractor, another requirement for graduation. On my big day, to exhibit my driving prowess, I put the gear shift into reverse and backed the tractor into the school pond.

Not all was lost, however, because this is when I had my first formal training in flower arranging. I loved every minute of those classes: creating centerpieces, filling vases with roses, and handcrafting corsages. But on graduation day, I was given an unsigned diploma. Having discovered my passion, I furthered my education by attending design school in Boston the next year. Now my quest for a life devoted to working with flowers had begun.

After working for several well-known flower shops in New York and Massachusetts, I was appointed director of Temple Galleries, a large floral decorating and gift shop in suburban Boston. During this period, I was a frequent guest lecturer at design schools across the country and was ultimately honored by the American Academy of Florists and selected as Chairperson. I became a spokesperson for the American Floral Marketing Council, doing public service and informational programs for radio and television.

During the second Nixon inauguration, I was invited by Mr. Elmer "Rusty" Young, then florist at the White House, to assist in decorations for the inaugural balls. Several times during the remainder of his term

Dottie Temple in the White House flower shop cooler.

in office, I helped with flower arrangements for official events. With the Ford inauguration, I was named Society of American Florists Liaison to the White House. In this capacity, I assisted in procuring floral material for use at the White House at Christmas, for State Dinners, and for other official functions. Eventually, I was called upon to design and create flower arrangements for various events, working with the White House staff.

This relationship continued through the Carter administration, when I was given the enjoyable task of designing many State Dinners and the Christmas decorations. During these years, we used the talent of numerous volunteers from within the flower world as well as private citizens. In early 1981, as the Carters were getting ready to leave the White House, it was suggested to Nancy Reagan that she might wish to hire me to replace Rusty Young, who was nearing retirement. I was interviewed by Mrs. Reagan and joined the White House staff right after the assassination attempt on the President. The next several years proved to be the most exciting and hectic in my life.

Along with all of the official events that called for floral decorations, our flower shop had to furnish the family quarters on the second and third floors with arrangements. The President and Mrs. Reagan were extremely charming and gracious and appreciative of all our efforts. Everyone on the Residence staff was very professional and a delight to work with. Our jobs were interdependent; chefs, ushers, butlers, maids, carpenters, electricians—in all, eighty-six people were dedicated to making the decor and ambience at the White House nearly perfect for the First Family and the many hundreds of dignitaries who visited throughout the year.

In this book, I will reveal how I helped to create this magnificent atmosphere at 1600 Pennsylvania Avenue through floral design and display. I hope to help you enhance your own individual style with touches of inspiration from the White House—a style that is simple and uncontrived, yet elegant enough to grace a city penthouse, a Federal town house, or a suburban home filled with the life of a family; flowers in a truly American style.

Oh, by the way, that diploma from my school days? Rex Scouten, the Chief Usher at the White House, called me into his office one day and gave me a package. It was my signed diploma with a letter of congratulations (thirty-nine years later!), stating that I had obviously succeeded in my chosen career even without knowing how to glaze a greenhouse or drive a tractor. ✍

THE FLOWER SHOP AT
1600 PENNSYLVANIA AVENUE

Imagine starting a new job in the
most celebrated house in the world

 and realizing that your floral arrangements will be displayed for the thousands of visitors who tour this national treasure each year. From my first day at the White House, I never lost that feeling of awe, knowing that my arrangements were to grace the very rooms in which Thomas Jefferson, Abraham Lincoln, Teddy Roosevelt, and John F. Kennedy had shaped our nation's history. That inspiration helped me through the countless hours preparing for a State Dinner, the early mornings before a Cabinet breakfast meeting, and the monumental work needed to create a perfect White House Christmas.

Until recent years, White House events of every kind were carefully supervised by the Department of State. The Secretary of State delegated this to a subordinate, for many years Alvey Adee. When he died, the Department of Protocol took over the responsibility. Toward the close of the twentieth century, the job shifted to the East Wing or First Lady's office staff and came under the jurisdiction of the social secretary. In a manuscript seating chart of a Lincoln dinner, White House customs for more than a century are illustrated. The President sits across from the First Lady. Other guests are seated on each side of them by official rank, in descending order. At each end of the table are the President's secretaries. The great plateau was used in the center, filled by now with fresh flowers sometimes frosted with gold paper doilies. At each man's place was a boutonniere and at each woman's a stiff nosegay with long streamers, both made in the greenhouse and both considered "favors."

In my early days as Chief Floral Decorator of the Executive Mansion, I usually started work at about 6:00 A.M., when I had the joyful task of selecting the most fabulous flowers, bursting with color, that the Washington flower market had to offer. To find unusual varieties, I often expanded my flower sources to Baltimore and New York. Once I had established a network by visiting all of the superior flower purveyors, I ordered flowers and foliage to be delivered to me, frequently phoning in my orders at the end of the day, after my staff had left for home. When the flowers arrived at the White House gate the next morning, they were always checked by guard dogs for suspicious material.

I reported to work every day at the flower shop, which is located on the ground floor of the White House, directly under the north portico. The White House flower shop operates under the National Park Service and has its space on the ground floor along with the main kitchen, carpenter shop, and the Office of the Curator. On the south side of the downstairs corridor are the China, Vermeil, and Map rooms and the Diplomatic Reception Room, where visiting diplomats ceremoniously present their credentials to the President.

The White House flower shop had four full-time employees and called upon a number of volunteer florists to assist at labor-intensive events such as State Dinners and on major holidays such as Christmas and Easter. The volunteers are generally representatives of different floral organizations, who pay all of their own expenses and must obtain a security clearance. They are always thrilled to be asked to donate their time, and when these "alumni" meet years later, they fondly recall their hectic "tenure" at the White House.

The flower shop was equipped much like a commercial florist. Each staff member had his or her own workbench where personal tools such as shears, knives, and wire picks were stored. There was room under each bench to hold floral foam and supplies. There was a sink nearby for filling containers with water. Our ribbons and plastic or glass liners were kept in wall storage units. Once the flowers arrived from the wholesaler, they were cut, placed in buckets of preservative to condition them, and then kept in the large walk-in cooler (which never seemed large enough) located at the back of the room. In this cooler we would also store our completed arrangements on steel shelving until they were ready for placement in the various rooms upstairs.

An important daily ritual performed by a member of the flower department staff was a walk-through of the State Floor rooms and offices and the Family Quarters to remove any wilting flowers, add water, and

check the overall condition of every arrangement. Generally, the flowers would need changing twice a week to keep them looking fresh. This run-through in the downstairs areas was completed before the public tours began at 8:00 A.M. On a typical day, with no significant social events, we were responsible for checking from seventy-five to a hundred arrangements. Many arrangements were quite large and placed on pier tables and mantelpieces, while others were petite enough for the First Lady's bedside table.

As a rule, our floral professionals were kept extremely busy placing flowers in all of the public rooms in the White House, the Family Quarters, the East and West wing offices and reception areas, the Navy Mess, Camp David (when the First Family was in residence), and *Air Force One*. We also provided the red, white, and blue wreaths placed at the Tomb of the Unknown Soldier and funeral flowers for statesmen and other dignitaries, as well as the memorial wreaths at the gravesites of all former Presidents.

ABOVE: *For a very large event, the flower shop staff is kept busy moving fresh flowers and other material from outside holding refrigerator trucks on the driveway of the White House to the ground floor, where they can be arranged.*

BELOW: *Betty Ford holds a breakfast meeting with Naval Aide Lieutenant Commander Stephen Todd at Camp David. Their worktable is tastefully decorated with a simple bowl of yellow and white marguerites and carnations.*

ABOVE LEFT: *A portrait of Luci Baines and Lynda Bird Johnson in front of hand-painted antique wallpaper and a silver champagne bucket. The flowers are very lifelike silk roses, lilies, iris, and delphinium.*

ABOVE RIGHT: *Jacqueline Kennedy is served a slice of birthday cake in the White House theater during a surprise birthday party she gave for her social secretary, Nancy Turnure. The sumptuous flowers at the buffet table include gerbera, snapdragons, and carnations.*

The great interest today in different species of flowers for White House arrangements was not entirely unfamiliar to early White House gardeners. While fresh-cut flowers were not used in the White House before the James Buchanan administration, just prior to the Civil War, blooming plants in tubs were often brought out to decorate events. Nourished in an orangery, which was a greenhouse without overhead glass but with tall windows to the south, the favorites were the camellias and sesanquia. These were brought into the house and lined up in the halls as early as the 1830s for decoration.

The White House is run like a five-star hotel, and the Chief Usher acts as the hotel's executive director, overseeing the entire establishment. While I was Chief Floral Decorator, the Chief Usher was Rex Scouten. Every Monday morning at 9:00 A.M. the heads of all the departments, including plumbing, carpentry, housekeeping, and groundskeeping, plus the executive chef, head butler, and curator would meet to review the weekly schedule of events. Mr. Scouten also issued a comprehensive monthly calendar detailing the exact times and locations of various events on the President's and First Lady's social schedules. He coordinated all of our efforts so that our work would appear seamless and perfect, even for the largest festivity.

The paperwork involved in maintaining a successful array of flower accents throughout the White House and beyond its environs is rather monumental. Time sheets, orders, invoices, planning charts, preliminary design sketches and photos, meetings with the First Lady and social secretaries, and logistical schedules for major events often extended my workdays until the evening hours. Billing for the many types of events was handled differently. Everyday flower arrangements in public settings are part of the Department of Interior budget, since the White House is under the auspices of the National Park Service, whereas all of the arrangements for a State Visit are paid for by the State Department.

This is one of two Nubian torchères that flank the North Portico door. They were frequently enhanced with half-round stands on which we placed seasonal plants and flowers. Here I designed a spring display of caladium, primula, hyacinths, tulips, azaleas, and marguerites.

RIGHT: *President Gerald Ford escorts Queen Elizabeth II through the center hall of the second-floor Residence, followed by Mrs. Ford and Prince Philip (not shown). They pass a lovely arrangement of roses, daisies, lilies, and delphiniums en route to a reception held before a State Dinner in honor of the Queen on July 7, 1976.*

BELOW: *In the old family dining room off the cross hall, President George Bush entertains Amir Sheikh Jabir al-Ahmad of Kuwait. The rich, bare table makes a stark surface on which a bold display of hot pink gerbera, pink and red carnations, and snapdragons is set.*

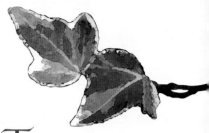

The challenge and excitement that preceded a summit or high-profile State Visit began more than a month in advance with the issuing of a comprehensive calendar of exact dates, times, and locations of the activities. Then our pace in the White House flower shop kicked into high gear. Sometimes the calendars were updated as often as three or four times a day. I would begin my planning by meeting with the Executive White House Chef about the menu—particularly the food presentation and colors, so that the choice of flowers would be compatible.

If the event was to honor a foreign dignitary, I would make a call to that country's desk at the State Department to check if there might be any allergies or any reasons why a specific flower might be inappropriate. For instance, in Japan all white flowers are used only for funerals, and Italian visitors would associate chrysanthemums with the same meaning. On the other hand, some political figures had floral preferences, and many heads of state were orchid collectors. President François Mitterrand of France loved roses, Prime Minister Margaret Thatcher fancied anemones, and West German Chancellor Helmut Schmidt's wife was particularly fond of geraniums.

President Lyndon Johnson in the Aspen Lodge at Camp David in Maryland meeting with Ambassador Ellsworth Bunker, Secretary of Defense Clark Clifford, Secretary of State Dean Rusk, General Earl Wheeler, William Bundy, and Walter Rostow. The flowers typify a handsome, informal coffee table arrangement.

The White House seemed vast when it was built, certainly larger than any house in the United States before the Civil War. Those who ventured to the roof could look out over Washington and see the ambitious and gardenesque city George Washington had demanded and seen begun. With its green Mall and groves, Washington itself becomes a flower arrangement in the spring, with redbud, dogwood, purple magnolia, and other flowering trees massed along its streets and through the parks, themselves crammed with tulips and daffodils. Each year the city waits for the cherry blossoms to bloom on the trees Helen Taft planted along the Tidal Basin; the trees were a gift from the mayor of Tokyo; sometimes the trees bloom too soon and are nipped by frost, but more often they splendidly announce spring. An ancient magnolia tree planted by Andrew Jackson thrives against the columns of the South Portico, faithfully blooming each June as if to close spring in a glorious display and introduce summer.

The Rose Garden, to the west, is just outside the Oval Office and cabinet room. First on the site was a rose garden under glass in the conservatory. Mrs. Roosevelt's colonial garden was nearby. Ellen Axson Wilson, President Woodrow Wilson's first wife, conceived of a rose garden on this site immediately upon moving to the White House in 1913. She and the celebrated landscape architect George Burnap designed a garden of "rooms" created by high privet hedges. Within each room were plantings of different flowers, but the climax was a long allée of roses highlighted by a statue of Pan playing his pipes. She loved flowers and envisioned afternoon teas here, with a long lattice wall for the display of her and her friends' paintings.

After her death at the White House in 1914, the garden was maintained, but no special attention was given to it for many years. In 1962, President John F. Kennedy, encouraged by horticulturist Rachel Lambert Mellon and her colleague Perry Wheeler, sponsored a redesign of the garden, which he wished to be both a garden filled with flowers and a green carpet where hundreds could gather for a bill signing, presentation, or speech. As such it has remained, although today luxurious shade precludes the presence of many roses. White House florists rarely cut from the flower gardens for their arrangements.

The tablescape would assume a theme at my initial meeting with the First Lady. Along with her social secretary, we would decide upon the china service, crystal, linens, and color scheme for the centerpieces. Several days later, I would unveil an original floral design for the approval of the First Lady. Since she was my only "customer," I had to be sure to keep her happy. The public areas were also filled with arrangements carrying over the same floral theme. I always called in the White House photo office to document the completed tablesetting, with fresh flowers, as it would appear the night of the dinner. This was essential in case I was unable to work during the State Visit; then another member of my staff could re-create the arrangements that the First Lady had approved.

At the designated time, the arrangements would be brought up from the flower shop to the State Floor and put into place. The First Lady would usually come down for a last-minute look, sometimes combined with a press viewing and photo shoot. My staff would have an early dinner and wait for the State Dinner to end and the guests to be seated in the East Room for the entertainment. Then we would go up the back stairs (since the White House has only one service elevator and it was used mainly by the kitchen staff) and hand-carry all of the arrangements from the dining room to the flower shop to store the flowers in the cooler overnight. By this time, it would be 10:00 or 10:30 P.M. The following day these flowers would be recut and reconditioned for use in other areas of the White House complex. After starting our day at seven in the morning, too tired to sustain our exhilaration, we would all go home for a much-needed rest. ✍

LEFT: *Occasionally for State Visits there would be several overflow tables from the State Dining Room set up in the Chinese Garden Room, an area at the end of the ground-floor corridor adjacent to the covered walkway connecting the Residence and the West Wing. Here, in that setting, I am putting the finishing touches on a simple low arrangement of pink shaded gerbera in a vermeil bowl for a State Dinner in honor of King Juan Carlos of Spain. Note the very tall candles. They are 24 inches tall and cast a most flattering light on all those seated at the table.*

ABOVE: *President Bill Clinton addresses the attendees at a State Dinner honoring Premier Zhu Rhongji of China. On each table, four tall tapers accent low round bowls of red and yellow parrot tulips and peachy yellow and white roses set in the center of deep red tablecloths set with the Reagan Presidential Service.*

BELOW: *Chief Floral Decorator Nancy Clarke, my assistant while I was at the White House, fixes gold pillar candles interspersed in long, low arrangements of blue hydrangeas and yellow roses for the Euro-Atlantic Partnership Council Summit Dinner in April 1999.*

Step-by-Step

INTRODUCTION

of the Executive Mansion was as well stocked with equipment and tools as any busy metropolitan florist. The tools I relied on most often were a very sharp knife and a very sharp pair of scissors. (Make sure yours fit comfortably in your hand.) Of course, I also used wire cutters when an event at the White House required dry arrangements or wreaths and garlands.

Occasionally I needed "cut and hold" scissors, which do just as the name implies; their 2-inch blade can handle woody stems up to ⅜ inch thick. These are made by the same people who make Swiss Army knives. I also liked to use serrated scissors to cut large, tough flower stems.

The drawers under my workbench in the flower room also had plenty of arranging aids such as three-inch wired picks (toothpick-like objects with a long piece of wire) that make it easy to attach fruit, berries, nuts, or any other accent material to your arrangements. These picks also come in 6-inch lengths and are wonderful when constructing large topiaries. Spool wire has many uses, such as binding two or more sprigs of greens or flowers together, affixing greens to a wire base for a wreath or basket, and wrapping flowers and greens together on a rope to make a garland. Don't forget the straight wire is great for bows, boutonnieres, or wedding bouquets when you need to wire each flower separately.

When I created an arrangement in a low, shallow container, such as a dinner centerpiece, pin holders made the task much easier. The flower stems are impaled on the points of the pins to hold them in place. I recommend two sizes to begin with a 1½- to 2½-inch round or oval shape. Then other sizes can be added, up to a 4-inch-round holder. You will need to use posy clay, which comes in a roll and is very sticky, to anchor the pin holder to the bottom of the container. If you don't want to adhere posy clay directly to the bottom of your vessel, try using a tuna can as a liner and placing the pin holder in it.

For more traditional, elaborate floral decorations, I relied exclusively on water-soaked floral foam to position flower stems. You can insert them at various angles so that the flower heads can be appreciated equally from all sides of a display while creating a gentle, curved overall outline. Foam-based arrangements generally do not last as long as those in water, so you must add water with a spray bottle, long-spouted watering can, or turkey baster each day. ✍

Silver Ice Bucket

3 stems of cut amaryllis
6 to 7 strands of raffia
Floral foam
Moss

1. Cut the foam to fit the ice bucket and cover with fresh green moss.

2. Tie the three amaryllis flower heads together, just at the base of the blossoms, with raffia strands.

3. Make a loose bow of the raffia and leave longish ends.

4. Poke a hole in the foam just large enough to insert the three amaryllis stems. You may first fill each stem with water and stop up the ends with a piece of foam or cotton. This is a good way to see that hollow-stemmed flowers have enough water. If the hole was cut too large and the stems do not stand upright, push small pieces of foam or moss in alongside the stems to stabilize them. This same method works for many types of flowers, such as carnations, roses, alstromeria, and bouvardia.

FRENCH TOLE CONTAINER

This arrangement is very beautiful and extremely long lasting when made with freeze-dried roses. One relatively new entry into the flower world is freeze-dried stems. Roses, gardenias, and sunflowers, among others, are put through a machine-drying process that renders them soft and pliable and capable of lasting for months. They may be used in the same way as any fresh flowers.

Bunch (24 leaves) of galyx leaves
24 leonides roses
3 pheasant feathers
Floral foam
Moss

1. Fill a tole container with foam and cover with moss.

2. Edge the container with a flat ring of the galyx leaves sticking straight out, parallel to the top of the container.

3. Make a ring of roses around the edge of the container, just inside the galyx leaves. Then continue with a second, smaller ring, and a third, working into the center. Round the flowers up a bit as you complete each row. The top should be nicely rounded.

4. Trim the feathers as needed and insert into the center.

DRAMATIC BLACK POTTERY VASE

This arrangement perfectly exemplifies the fact that there is no such thing as clashing colors in flowers. The pinks, reds, and burgundy blend in perfectly with the purple and blues of the lisianthus and hydrangea, all softened by the touch of cream freesia and yellow oncidium.

> *7 yellow oncidium orchids*
> *5 cream freesia*
> *8 purple and white lisianthus*
> *3 pinky red tulips*
> *5 hot pink roses*
> *5 gloriosa lilies*
> *5 stems of "Autumn Joy" sedum*
> *2 large hydrangea heads*
> *3 peach tulips*

1. The first step and real secret of this simple arrangement is to establish the size of your arrangement by placing a few of the most slender flowers in a rough arc in the vase.

2. Fill in with the remaining flowers so that the colors and textures are interspersed and not clustered. Be sure to push some stems deeper into the vase with others poking out higher so that the arrangement doesn't appear flat but three-dimensional.

Nautilus Vase on a Mantel

This lovely shell vase is perfect for a fireplace mantel setting. Because of the container's curved shape, the arrangement tends to be one-sided.

6 peach tulips

4 calla lilies

4 peach roses

4 stars of Bethlehem

4 veronicas

Eucalyptus

2 white bouvardia

3 St. John's wort

7 strands of variegated ivy

Floral foam

Moss

1. Fill the vase with foam and cover the edges with moss.

2. Insert the tulips into the left side of the shell and add the calla lilies to spill way out over the edge.

3. Create a dramatically tall center with the roses, stars of Bethlehem, and veronicas.

4. To add balance, repeat Step 2, using the same number of tulips and calla lilies on the right side. Then add the bouvardia.

5. Trail some ivy and St. John's wort from the shell's lip for a graceful touch.

Diane Bowl
for a Luncheon Table

5 mini terra-cotta-colored
   calla lilies
3 Leonides roses
4 peach roses
2 peach tulips
5 white bouvardia
4 veronicas
4 stars of Bethlehem
2 St. John's worts
3 strands of variegated ivy
Several branches of eucalyptus
Floral foam
Moss

1. Fill the bowl with foam and cover the edges with moss.

2. Place the calla lilies in the foam, angling gracefully to establish the height of your arrangement. Then use two more lilies to establish the width.

3. Making sure the arrangement is even on all sides, add the roses, tulips, bouvardia, veronicas, St. John's wort, and the rest of the calla lilies.

4. Finish the arrangement by adding the slender veronicas and stars of Bethlehem, the ivy, and the eucalyptus.

Here is a radiant, majestic centerpiece for a State Dinner honoring Prime Minister Menachem Begin of Israel in April 1980. The gold drapes and chairs with the gilded architectural accents in this impressive room set the color scheme for the yellow spring daffodils in glass bowls.

Historic how-to
CARTER STATE DINNER CENTERPIECE

To make this type of arrangement, you can find thin, almost invisible
Lucite rods to elevate a container or floral foam adapter into which
flowers may be arranged more gracefully, above the
rest of the arrangement.

Plastic saucer	*Glass rose bowl*
Lucite pedestal	*Floral foam*
Mixed daffodils	*Moss*
Pin holder	*Posy clay*

1. Fill the saucer with water-soaked foam after attaching it to the Lucite pedestal with posy clay. Cover the foam with moss and arrange the daffodils as if they were growing from it. You may want to soften the look a bit with some natural foliage.

2. Place the pin holder in the bottom of the rose bowl and fasten it with posy clay.

3. Insert foliage in and around the pin holder to conceal it, and then arrange the daffodils in the pin holder. In this example, they are very tightly grouped.

4. Place the rose bowl on top of the saucer and fasten with posy clay.

GUIDELINES FOR GRAND DESIGN

Jacqueline Kennedy made many long-standing changes in the White House, from initiating the most ambitious and authentic redecoration of the Executive Mansion to influencing the daily task of displaying flowers in public areas. She was the first in her position as First Lady to hire a person specifically as the White House florist, Rusty Young, and she insisted that only certain antique vases, bowls, and tureens be used in certain rooms because of their historical significance.

Mrs. Kennedy's initiative of cataloging containers and instructions for their placement remains in use today. Sometimes subsequent First Ladies, along with the current chief Floral Decorator, make their own decisions about where vases and other decorative items are placed. However, her

Not all presidents and first ladies were interested in flowers. Eleanor Roosevelt, for example, took little part in their placement, and flower arrangements under FDR tended to be very simple, of the sort one found in florist shops of the time. She did like a corsage and, according to the custom of her day, was presented with many of them. The President and First Lady had both shown an interest in gardening before their White House years, but never had the White House seen two busier people than these. Mrs. Roosevelt's approach to the fine points of White House living was to streamline, reducing needs to their smallest number. Flower arranging was not a high priority.

timeless mark on floral design at the White House is best appreciated by examining the types of floral arrangements she introduced. During Mrs. Kennedy's tragically short tenure, the stiff, fan-shaped form of arrangements from the preceding century gave way to a looser, French-influenced style with colorful mixtures of different blossoms. The stems were cut to varying lengths to build massed bouquets of graceful curves, while the palette was always coordinated with the paintings and silk-screened wall hangings in each room. Every First Lady since the Kennedy administration has continued to utilize Jefferson-inspired round tables for an informal style of entertaining at State Dinners.

The wonderful thing I love about flower arranging is the opportunity to create art that directly connects us to the natural world. Because flowers are so adaptable yet exquisite in themselves, one can create a captivating work of art without too many constraints or rules. Even a modest amount of inspiration can yield a lovely bouquet for any occasion.

As with any craft, there are some guidelines to consider to gain the most from flower arranging, but they shouldn't get in the way of express-

BELOW: *An interesting combination of two tropical flowers, allium gigantum and waterlilies, created for a midsummer night's State Dinner during the Carter administration.*

ing your own individual style. I find that my floral arrangements are mostly adaptations of the traditional European style. Such arrangements were originally fairly dense. However, today a looser, less studied look is more compatible with a modern lifestyle. The overall appearance is relaxed, with the use of space around the flowers an important element.

Context—the occasion for and surroundings of your arrangement—is practically everything. At the White House, I planned more elaborate floral displays for State Visits and their extravagant receptions than I would for a presidential cabinet luncheon. The arrangement should be integrated into the room decor by reinforcing either a formal atmosphere or a casual feeling. The appropriateness of an arrangement also takes its cue from the container. A Federal-style room can accept silver or Chinese export ware with most likely a massed arrangement, whereas a country kitchen or dining room would more likely call for a spatterware mug or copper mixing bowl. Remember, the purpose for creating a floral arrangement is to add another beautiful element to your entertaining.

ABOVE: *In the late spring and early fall in Washington, D.C., the weather is delightful for entertaining outside, even for a formal State Dinner. Here is the table-setting for a dinner in honor of President Ferdinand Marcos of the Philippines. Vermeil bamboo-style containers were placed on mirror plateaus. The candles are held in handblown glass votive holders on glass rods inserted into the foam, and the flowers are a symphony of white with white liatris, gerberas, tuberoses, ixia, stars of Bethlehem, and hybrid lilies.*

RIGHT: *At a State Dinner for King Hassan II of Morocco, Mrs. Carter relaxes for a moment at her table. Because she was very fond of tropical flowers and the after-dinner entertainment was ballet, I chose a streletzia centerpiece to extend the feeling of physical grace and beauty to the dining experience.*

ABOVE: *President Jimmy Carter and his wife, Rosalynn, enjoying a State Dinner conversation with President Nicolae Ceauşescu of Romania around a table centered with a large wide-mouthed glass bowl of floating camellias. Mrs. Carter also wore a lovely camellia at her wrist.*

Color usually makes the strongest impact in any arrangement. It was an essential aspect of my decision in designing floral decorations in every room of the White House. I always conferred with the First Lady and her social secretary right at the outset of planning for an event to decide on a color scheme before selecting the specific flowers. The material of the container, such as precious metal or decorated porcelain, also needs to be consistent with the table linens and even the room color.

Fortunately, for large sit-down dinners where many centerpieces are required, the neutral-colored walls and gold drapes of the State Dining Room allow for a wide array of flowers and containers. At home, I favor the Flemish mixture of colors, which melds a variety of earthy colors and flowers with the addition of fruits and vegetables. For a novice arranger, it may be safer to begin with two or three colors such as adjacent color-wheel hues like orange/red, purple/blue, blue/green, or green/yellow.

Before Mrs. Kennedy moved into the White House, only white flowers were displayed in the Red Room because of its vivid walls. She suggested adding red peonies and red-flecked white rubrum lilies to add interest and pick up the new cerise hangings. For the Diplomatic Reception Room, Mrs. Kennedy persuaded the National Society of Interior Decorators to purchase and then donate to the White House an antique panoramic wallpaper of American landscapes in rich hues of greens, blues, golds, and browns. It provided a stunning backdrop to a galaxy of red, lavender, and yellow anemones or Duchess spoon chrysanthemums with bronze and red pompoms. The yellow tones also complement the gold-and-white color scheme of the upholstered furniture and rug.

So vivid was the color of the Red Room after President Harry Truman finished his major remodeling in 1952 that only white flowers were considered appropriate for use there. Several fresh arrangements were brought in each week, sometimes roses, sometimes carnations. Truman's remodeling of the White House to rebuild it within the original walls, from 1948 to 1952, notably corresponded with the years of the Marshall Plan, when he was helping to rebuild war-torn Europe. The "restoration" was drastic, but it ensured the White House would continue as the home of the Presidents. This Red Room decor is fairly representative of what President Truman did to the White House. It would be Mrs. Kennedy, a decade later, who would begin transforming the rooms into historical settings, which they remain today.

The Red Room is seen here during the Clinton administration. The small export bowl holds a lush mixture of open pink roses and miniature calla lilies. The soft colors work very well against the deep-hued wall covering.

Proportion: A rule of thumb that may be helpful to the beginner is that the flowers in an arrangement should be approximately 1 ½ times the largest dimension of the container. This is so the flowers are not overshadowed by their holder or do not appear to overtake the container. The Blue Room, completely redecorated in 1972 by Pat Nixon in its original French Empire style, contains several vases, urns, and bowls. The large, oval room has antique English marble-topped console tables on which low Chinese export bowls are displayed. My choice for these containers is a mass arrangement in the Williamsburg style, made of lilies, roses, bouvardia, and some interesting contrasting foliage. These follow the shape of the bowl and do not overpower the table on which it rests.

Another basic rule of proportion I used regularly at the White House is the "elbow rule": When you are seated, place your elbow on the table, point your arm upward, and bend your wrist. The floral centerpiece should either be above your wrist or below, but not exactly at the bend or it will fall at eye level and block the view of dinner guests across the table. Finally, another simple but sophisticated example of maintaining the right proportion is filling a bud vase with one or two stems. Nancy Reagan loved the look I fashioned on her dressing table with a collection of dissimilar glass bud vases filled with her favorites: tuberoses, sweet peas, lilies of the valley, and roses.

Gorgeous chrysanthemums, lilies, pompoms, snapdragons, and roses in a Chinese export bowl become the focal point on this marble-topped table in the oval-shaped Blue Room. The round arrangement echoes the shape of the table and the curve of the walls.

The President's Dining Room in the Residence after renovation by President and Mrs. Bill Clinton. The centerpiece is a traditional oval arrangement on this rectangular table. The flowers—red carnations, Queen Anne's lace, and yellow and red parrot tulips—are in a vermeil tureen. On the mantel are similar arrangements.

A well-designed arrangement also depends on balance, both visual and physical. Obviously, the weight and mechanics of a container filled with flowers must be considered so that it does not become top-heavy or lopsided and fall over. In addition, the overall appearance should be symmetrically balanced. I always place the largest blooms at the base or focal point of the arrangement, surrounded by spiky smaller flowers and buds. Especially for the mantelpiece topiaries I created at Christmas and the large spring arrangements for the cross halls in the White House, I was careful to add sufficient weight to the liners and plenty of framing for the floor versions.

Texture also plays an important role in a successful flower arrangement. It adds another dimension to our appreciation of the flowers by stimulating our sense of touch through the surface quality of leaves, stems, and the petals themselves. Mixing textures such as velvety roses, shiny camellia foliage, and bits of moss and twigs gives the arrangement a natural look, while mixing yellow roses, ixia, a few smoky leaves of dusty miller, some pale green artichokes, and a couple of waxy yellow green and orange miniature peppers evokes a feeling of opulence just bursting with texture and color.

Ceremony is infrequent and even unusual in American culture. Apart from the courtroom, there is little official ceremony and all is subject to change. What of the White House? The grand East Room was built for ceremony. President George Washington called it the "Audience Room," where presumably he was to receive petitions from citizens; more significantly, he was to receive bills brought there and presented to him by the Congress, all of its members in attendance. This brings to mind platforms covered with rich carpets and—dare I say it?—a throne. Jefferson buried these sorts of grand ideas with his inauguration in 1801. The East Room was unfinished when he moved to the White House, and he left it that way. It would be destroyed, still unfinished, when the British burned the house in 1814, and it would not be completed until Andrew Jackson did so in 1829, thirty-seven years after Washington approved the building of the room.

Presidential funerals at the White House have been few, but they started early, in 1841 with William Henry Harrison, who died unexpectedly after only a month in office. The house was draped in black. After all the preparations were made, the President's coffin (there were actually three, nested inside one another) was placed on a table in the entrance hall, then moved to the East Room for the funeral.

Abraham Lincoln's funeral was next. When two thousand invited guests crammed together on shallow bleachers in the East Room and the preacher rambled on, the room became oppressively hot and the pungent perfume of many flowers hung in the air. Of the presidents who have died in office, only James Garfield did not lie in state at the White House. This was because a major work of interior decoration was in process and the house was torn up.

From the very elaborate decorations at presidential funerals in the nineteenth and early twentieth centuries, custom has simplified the extent of mourning that is used. When President John F. Kennedy lay in state in the East Room in 1963, swags of black crepe ringed the three mighty chandeliers, only a suggestion of the far more elaborate drapery used in earlier times.

Although the fragrance of fresh flowers seems a rather easy asset to exploit, it can be taken for granted—with rather unpleasant consequences. I remember a story told to me by Letitia Baldrige, Jackie Kennedy's social secretary, about the time when Mrs. Kennedy hired the famous muralist Bernard Lamont to paint a mural of the U.S. Virgin Islands on the wall of the White House swimming pool. For one reason or another, he refused to eat the food that the Executive Chef, René Verdon, would prepare, and brought his own each day, consisting of a French baguette, salami, ham, and French cheese. After a week or so, everyone noted a very strange odor in the public rooms on the first floor. The entire staff searched and searched but could not find the answer to the problem.

Until one day, when someone discovered that Bernard had been putting his leftover lunches in the flower shop's walk-in cooler. The strong odor of the cheese and meats had permeated the floral arrangements in the cooler, and after they had been brought into the warmth of the first floor, the "new" smells won out! Moral: Forget the salami in your arrangements! (Ethylene gases from fruits and vegetables in your refrigerator can kill your flowers, too.)

Chief Florist Rusty Young, Julia Clements, Lady Seaton from London, and I admire a lovely porcelain bowl filled with roses, white stock, and snapdragon in the library on the ground floor of the White House in 1976.

Tools of the Trade

Following is a list of tools and materials that I find essential.

Floral knife: Probably the most important piece of equipment for a flower arranger, this sharp knife should fit comfortably into the palm of your hand. I prefer a Swiss Army knife because it keeps its edge and is reliably strong.

Floral cutting shears: Almost as important as the knife, these scissors should be easy to hold and kept very sharp to make a clean cut. Remember to cut flower stems under water whenever possible.

Cut-and-hold scissors: These shears have a 2-inch blade and do what the name implies: they hold and cut the stem at the same time. I use them to cut soft or woody stems up to ⅜ inch thick.

Pin holders: These are wonderful to use when you are creating an arrangement in a low, shallow container. The flowers are impaled on the sharp pins to hold them in place. I recommend two sizes to begin with, 1½ to 2½ inches and a 4-inch round or oval.

Posy clay: This comes in a roll and is very sticky. It is used to anchor the pin holder to the bottom of your container.

3-inch wire picks: These are like small green or natural-colored wooden toothpicks with a wire attached. They are used to attach fruit, berries, nuts, or any other small object into an arrangement. They also come in a 6-inch length and are very useful when making Christmas wreaths or other large arrangements.

Spool wire: This has many uses: to bind two or more sprigs of greens or flowers together, to affix mixed greens to a wire base when making a wreath, to make a hanger for the back of a wreath, and to bind greens and flowers together on a rope when making a garland.

Straight wire: I sometimes use this wire when making bows or boutonnieres. In a wedding bouquet, each and every flower is attached with straight wire to achieve the desired shape and size of the handheld arrangement.

Wire cutters: The perfect tool to use when working with silk or dried flower stems, such as those used in Christmas wreaths and garlands, or possibly when making flowers to wear.

Ribbon shears: These are great for cutting ribbons when making bows, or they can be used for trimming leaves and petals.

Pruning shears: I use these heavy-duty scissors whenever I need to cut woody stems, such as fruit branches being forced in the spring, curly willow, or kiwi for dramatic accents.

Floral foam: A water-holding foam into which fresh flower stems are inserted.

Floral tape: This tape can be used in a couple of ways. First, I anchor floral foam to the base of containers with it. Stretched across the top of a container, it will keep the foam from slipping or popping out of your vase or basket. It also comes in a clear form, like Scotch tape, that can be criss-crossed over glassware to create a webbing to hold flower stems upright.

Flower food: This should be used in every container in which flowers are arranged. I have been pleased with the results that I get from a line of food manufactured in Holland, where so many of our imported flowers are grown.

Turkey baster: An old-fashioned turkey baster is ideal for adding water to or removing it from intricate arrangements.

Favorite Flowers—

These are some of my favorite flowers that I used most often in my signature White House arrangements.

Agapanthus and belladonna: These last nicely—usually about a week—when placed in water with preservative.

Alchemilla mollis: Cut these under cool running water and place in preservative before arranging. They will last about a week.

Alstromeria: After bringing these flowers home, cut the bottoms of the stems off and strip off all the leaves from the stems up to the point where the flowers branch out.

Amaryllis, delphiniums, and other hollow-stemmed flowers: These will last longer if you fill and plug the stems with floral foam or cotton before arranging in water. They will generally last as long as a potted flower.

Anemones: These should be placed in deep water after they have been cut and will last about a week in an arrangement; they do not survive well in floral foam.

Baby's breath: These should be put into about 3 inches of very hot water with preservative and a splash of bleach. You can detangle baby's breath by swishing it in water.

Brodeas: These can be placed in water after cutting and will last an average of four to five days.

Calla lilies: Cut the hollow stems with a sharp knife and place in cool water with preservative. They can last up to a week, depending on their degree of development.

Carnations: Cut them on an angle between the joints and place them in warm water until ready to arrange.

Clematis: Dip their stems into boiling water to help preserve them. They do not last long but are beautiful for short-term arrangements.

Columbines: These flowers last very well in copper or silver containers. Buds continue to open for seven to ten days.

Fruit branches and shrub roses: Peel and split their tough stems about 1 or 2 inches under water before immersing in shallow water to arrange. A forked branch wedged into a tall container will keep tall stems or branches in place.

Galyxes: Keep these wrapped in wax paper or in a plastic bag in the vegetable drawer of your refrigerator. These last surprisingly well, sometimes for several months.

Gardenias, camellias, and pansies: All of these benefit from immersion in water, head and all, for 2 to 3 hours.

Hydrangeas: First peel about 2 to 3 inches off of the stem and split the stem a little bit, then dip them into boiling water. They will last about five days in a wet arrangement or can be dried for a permanent arrangement.

Ivy: Cut vines last very well. If the stems are woody, hammer them a bit before placing them into water; if the leaves wilt, submerge the whole vine in water until it revives.

Ixia: Cut the stems and hammer them a bit to soften them. Once you have removed all of the leaves, place them into water and preservative. These are very long lasting flowers, from ten days to two weeks.

Lace flowers (scabiosa): Cut these under running water, and they should last a very long time, about ten days.

Lilacs: Their woody stems need to be hammered or split before you place them into conditioning solution.

Lilies: Always remove the pollen-covered stamens from each flower. The pollen stains clothing and tablecloths, and the lilies will last longer without their stamens. Blotting with sticky tape or a pipe cleaner may remove the pollen if it does get onto fabric.

Maidenhair ferns: Their stems are very tender, yet need to be cut and placed in water, but be careful not to crowd.

Mimosas: Always cut these in full bloom and place the stems into boiling water. The flower heads benefit from a spraying of cool water while in the arrangement.

Peonies: Place these in hot water after cutting. Take care to shake or pick off any ants before arranging.

Poppies, euphorbias, and other "bleeding" stem flowers: Place these into boiling water for a few seconds or touch the bottom of the stem to a flame before immersing in deep water.

Roses: Always cut them under cool running water and immerse them in water right before arranging. Remove all thorns and lower foliage, except for the top two or three leaf sets. To revive a wilted rose, plunge the stem into boiling water for a few seconds. The breeze from a hair dryer wafted over tightly closed roses will open them.

Sea holly: This can be either placed in water after cutting (to last about a week) or hung to dry for permanent arrangements.

Stars of Bethlehem (chincherinchee): As with all fresh flowers, cut the stem under water before arranging in water. Usually the florets will remain open for up to two weeks if you change the water often.

Sunflowers: Remove all of the foliage before placing these flowers into preservative. These generally last a long time, at least a week, or they may be dried by hanging, and then removing some petals for an interesting, weathered look.

Tuberoses: These are very long lasting if you remove all of the foliage below the water line. Usually all of the florets will open along the stem from the bottom up to the top. Remove any dead flowers to maintain the look of your arrangement.

Tulips: These continue to grow when placed in water. After picking or purchasing them, cut off the white part of the stem because it blocks water absorption. Wrap them tightly in wax paper, then in damp newspaper, and place in cool water to straighten the stems. If you want them to hang over the edge of a container, place them in a vase low enough to bend; they will harden off with the desired curvature.

Watsonias: Before preserving, cut the stems and remove all leaves. Removing the tips encourages the buds to open.

Zinnias: To keep these colorful summer flowers looking their best, push a straight pin into the stem just under the head and place into water. ✍

These elegant tulips drape languidly over the State Dining Room mantel in April 1982 to honor Queen Beatrix of the Netherlands during an event commemorating the three hundredth anniversary of trade relations between the United States and the Netherlands.

Step-by-Step

INTRODUCTION

When flowers were delivered to me

at the White House, everyone in the shop dropped everything he or she was doing to get the new flowers into water as soon as possible. In most cases, these flowers had come directly from the growers, looking underdeveloped and limp, and had never been in water. I hated to see a single beautiful bloom lost, so we wasted no time in conditioning them.

We stripped any leaves below what would become the water line in the arrangement and cut an inch off the bottom. In particular, cutting roses under warm water helps to avoid the possibility of air bubbles forming and rendering the stems unable to draw water. Generally, we plunged the flowers into well-scrubbed buckets about half filled with warm water and ¼ cup of flower preservative. Finally, we placed them in our shop cooler overnight to "harden off" before we worked them into arrangements the next day.

Foliage, even the less delicate type such as ferns, benefits from a short, thorough soaking in lukewarm water, since it absorbs liquid directly through its leaves. After an hour or two of soaking, we shook off the excess water and placed the foliage into a conditioning bucket, again being careful to remove any foliage that would be below the eventual water level. If you buy flowers from a florist or supermarket, chances are that they have gone through this conditioning process. Try not to drive around for very long with flowers in your car before going home; even a brief stay in a bitterly cold or very hot car can compromise their color and resilience. Remember always to keep your vases scrupulously clean by washing them with soap and water and rinsing with a mild bleach solution between uses.

Flower food was used in every container into which I placed fresh flowers at the White House. Our metal shop made custom-fitted liners for the most valuable vases so that the water and chemicals would not harm their inside surfaces. If you do not have a liner, often a drinking glass or plastic jar slipped into the vase will work just as well. ✿

THREE RECTANGULAR GLASS VASES

Cranberries, like polished stones and seashells, make good flower holders in clear glass. They grow under water in bogs and can therefore last in a vase with water for a long time.

3 bags of cranberries
2 large green calla lilies
Small purple calla lilies

1. Pour about an inch and a half of cranberries into the bottom of your container.

2. Place the stems one at a time into the berries and fill the berries in around the stems until the flowers are fairly secure. They may be adjusted as necessary by moving the stems around gently. This is one way to use a fairly large clear glass vase with very few flowers.

STONE VASES WITH MIRROR

2 square mirrors, approximately 12 by 12 inches

1 pink stone vase

1 amethyst vase

2 pink quartz candleholders

9 to 11 purple calla lilies

1 stem of lady's mantle

3 to 4 variegated ivy pieces, 5 to 6 inches long

Floral foam

Votive candle

2 polished pink stones

4 chunks amethyst

1. Fill the vases with water and place two stems of mini calla lilies in each, keeping the heights uneven. Then insert short bits of lady's mantle into each vase close to the edge of the container.

2. Fill one candleholder with foam and arrange with more calla lilies and lady's mantle. Light the votive candle in the other quartz holder and move the pieces around on the mirrors to get the best reflective effect.

3. Add in the ivy tendrils to the containers wherever they will look most effective.

4. Arrange the pink stones and chunks of amethyst around vases and candleholder.

HENS-AND-CHICKENS
TABLE WREATH

3 4-inch pots of hens and chickens
7 stems of gloriosa lilies
12-inch floral foam ring
Sheet moss
Flocked wire

1. Soak the floral foam ring in water with preservative and let it drain.

2. Remove the hens and chickens from their pots and wash the roots.

3. Making small slits in the foam, gently poke in the small plants' roots. Continue around the wreath frame until it is covered about two thirds of the way around. If some of the plants seem loose, make a hairpin shape out of wire and push through the center of the plant. Flocked wire works best for this since the flocking is slightly rough and holds much better in the foam.

4. Fill in any spaces in the wreath where the foam is exposed with bits of fresh sheet moss, also anchoring it with hairpins and covering the third that was left bare.

5. In this section make an arrangement with the gloriosa lilies, keeping some tall and others out to the sides and low to reflect their unusual growth pattern.

Stone Mortar and Pestle

4 hot pink celosia plumosas
2 orange celosia plumosas
4 hot pink crisata celosia
1 orange crisata celosia
3 hot pink nerines
3 orange chili peppers
2 stems of yellow ornamental pepper
1 stem of lady's mantle
Eucalyptus
Floral foam
Posy clay
Sheet moss

1. Soak the floral foam in water and preservative and anchor it to the inside of a Mexican stone mortar with posy clay. Cover with sheet moss.

2. Place the pink and orange celosia plumosas straight up in the center, mixing their colors; the hot pink ones should be about 12 to 13 inches tall, the orange about 10 inches tall. Then place one slightly to the left and another pink one slightly to the right.

3. Insert the larger, pink crisata celosia, and fill in the center with the orange crisata celosia.

4. Add 3 nerines, about 13 to 14 inches tall, into the center of the arrangement. Then add another 8- to 9-inch-tall nerine near the right rear and another to the left rear of the mortar.

5. Complete the striking array by filling in with multicolored peppers and short pieces of lady's mantle.

6. Finally, add the finishing touch with a few eucalyptus leaves.

SPLIT ASH BASKET

This wonderful split ash basket seemed to cry out to be filled with autumn's bounty.

5 to 6 tall branches of red and yellow crab apples

7 to 10 calicarpas with leaves removed

Osage oranges

4 oak hydrangeas on stem

1 to 2 branches of oak leaves

1 head of flowering kale

3 to 5 fern fronds

Floral foam

Bamboo sticks

1. Fill a basket liner with wet floral foam and place the crabapple branches in at angles to approximate a triangle, making sure that some curve over the edges and that short pieces are placed to fill in the central area. Add hydrangeas at various heights.

2. Push the bamboo sticks into the osage oranges and insert them into the arrangement.

3. Add the long, sweeping calicarpa branches, letting them trail all through the arrangement.

4. Achieve a sculpted look with a few branches of oak leaves.

5. Finally, place the flowering kale in low, front and center as the focal point. Place ferns over the edge of the basket.

President Reagan hosted a State Dinner for King Hussein and Queen Noor of Jordan in 1981
(Queen Noor is to his right). Here I used twelve to fifteen varying sizes and heights of clear
glass bud vases with roses, freesias, orchids, and stars of Bethlehem arranged on
a mirror plateau. This display does require quite a bit of work to get just the
right look from every seating angle.

Historic how-to

BUD VASE CENTERPIECE

This arrangement was created for a State Dinner honoring King Hussein of Jordan. Mrs. Reagan wanted something simple and sophisticated. She loved the look I fashioned on her dressing table—an array of dissimilar glass bud vases filled with different flowers. So I decided to expand upon this theme and contacted the National Association of Mirror Manufacturers, which was kind enough to have a series of fourteen beveled glass mirror plateaus made as a gift to the White House.

12 to 15 clear glass bud vases, different in shape and height
Several stems each of dendrobium, Queen Anne's lace, roses, bouvardia, freesia, or other white flowers
A round, beveled mirror (as at the White House) or a rectangular mirror tile
Several clear glass votive candleholders with candles

1. Fill the vases with water and preservative.

2. Tall bud vases look best when filled with one to two stems of a single type of white flower. Lower ones can accommodate two or three types.

3. The vases need to be moved around quite a bit to get a pleasant total look with adequate sight lines for all guests. This idea is much easier on a rectangular table since the vases may be staggered through the center of the table.

4. Place the clear votive candleholders (I used ribbed holders) among the vases and light the candles. The flames' reflection off of the mirror is dazzling.

Part of the celebrated Monroe French plateau cradles a vivid horizontal arrangement of white stock, lavender/blue anemones, white carnations, and chrysanthemums at a private dinner held in the Diplomatic Reception Room to honor Igor Stravinsky on January 18, 1962, during the Kennedy administration. Jacqueline Kennedy loved a "country estate" look to her arrangements.

KENNEDY GREAT PIER ARRANGEMENT

Especially for this priceless piece, a liner filled with foam was placed in the gilt base. Since this arrangement was used in the center of a long table, an elongated style was dictated.

White stock	Blue and lavender anemones
White carnations	Red carnations
White pompoms	

1. Establish the length of the arrangement in the container with the white stock, then use several stock to create the proper height and fill in with more through the front and back of the container.

2. Next insert the carnations and pompoms into the foam to make a background for the blue and lavender anemones. Since these are the focal point of the arrangement and they appear to recede under candlelight, it is necessary to give them a little help with pale shades or white when used under low light conditions.

3. Finally, a few red carnations add just the right color accent.

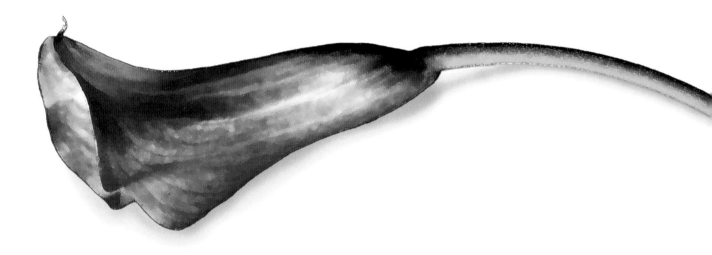

FORMAL CONTAINERS AND VASES

Selecting containers for floral arrangements at the White House is like a stroll through time, with almost any style or type of container available on a whim. From the magnificent French vermeil plateau purchased by President James Monroe to elegant Sèvres urns, gilded fruit baskets, or the beautiful and unique bamboo vermeil bowls made by Tiffany & Company during the Kennedy administration, I had a treasure of exquisite, priceless vases.

In general, as Chief Floral Decorator, I was allowed to use anything in the White House collection as long as the container was adequately fitted with a liner to protect each piece from excess water. These liners were custom-made in the White House metal shop to fit perfectly. Then, during the arranging process, these liners were filled with a

During Teddy Roosevelt's renovation of the White House, trophy heads hung over the mantels in the enlarged State Dining Room. A stereopticon slide of a dinner there for Prince Heinrich of Prussia shows a large curved table decorated with massive Victorian bouquets of pink roses and white carnations. Smilax garlands decorated the length of the table as well as the chandeliers and all the columns. The slide makers observed that "Prince Henry must have seemed to be having dinner in a Christmas tree."

water-holding foam as a design holder. In previous years, before the advent of foam, chicken wire had sometimes been crumpled up and placed in the container. However, the possibility of scratching the container was an ever-present problem.

For formal events, clear glass was not often used except in bud vases or fishbowl-type displays in which gardenias, open roses, or camellias were sometimes floated. One centerpiece that I remember as being especially brilliant was for a State Dinner given by President and Mrs. Carter in honor of Prime Minister Deng Xiaoping of China. Mrs. Carter's garden club friends from Georgia gathered hundreds of camellias and hand-delivered them to the White House, then assisted us in placing them in large glass bowls with floating candles on each table. They seemed exceptionally appropriate since the camellia originated in China and is the state flower of Georgia.

During my tenure at the White House, I frequently borrowed items from museum collections, such as Remington and Russell sculptures from the Amon Carter Museum in Texas, semiprecious gems from the Smithsonian Museum of Natural History, and Steuben glassware from the Corning Inc. company for use in centerpieces for State Dinners. One type of vase that was acquired as part of a gift from the New York World's Fair of 1939–1940 is an acid-etched urn with the Strawberry Mansion pattern, a stylized version of the Great Seal. Another frequently utilized set of containers comes from the White House Vermeil Collection, a selection of gilded pieces from the extensive silver-gilt bequest to the White House by Margaret Thompson Biddle in 1956. Chiefly English and French, the styles cover a wide time span from the Renaissance to the present day.

Princess Diana visits with Barbara Bush in the lovely Yellow Oval Room on the second floor of the Family Quarters during her trip to the United States in October 1990. In the background is an antique French porcelain basket filled with peach gerberas and roses. This delicate pedestal container was purchased during President John Tyler's administration as a fruit and cake basket. It has a blue-and-gold porcelain base with kneeling bisque angels supporting a gilt basket, donated to the White House collection by Tyler family descendants. (For instructions on re-creating this arrangement, see page 85.)

On many occasions, Edith Roosevelt requested that the Monroe plateau be divided into separate sections and filled with low, full arrangements of the same color of roses mixed with asparagus ferns. Tall, trumpet-shaped vases of silver or crystal with more roses and ferns were placed between the sections.

ABOVE: *The magnificent main table in the State Dining Room is set with the famous French plateau, commonly known as the Great Pier, purchased in Paris for President James Monroe in 1817. The gilt bronze plateau stretches more than 13 feet. It is the earliest surviving "container" bought for the White House. At its White House debut in 1818, it was stretched full length on the dining table, the lagoon of mirrors reflecting candles and arrangements of wax flowers. The early floral decorations for the plateau were wax flowers and greenery, bought with the plateau in Paris. Today the plateau is usually used in reduced size but, since the late 1850s, has always been decorated with fresh flowers. Here the tall basket centerpiece is filled with peach and white gerbera and orange lilies. The crystal bonbon dishes added by President John Tyler in 1864 are also filled at times, often with a combination of fruit and flowers.*

ABOVE: *A profusion of spring blossoms atop a section of the Monroe plateau: three griffins supporting a pierced basket. These snapdragons, lilies, jonquils, and marguerites were arranged during the Nixon administration.*

LEFT: *This is a Strawberry Mansion Urn made by Steuben Glass of Corning, N.Y., in 1939 for the Federal Building at the World's Fair in New York and transferred to the White House in 1941.*

This beautiful Sèvres urn-shaped pedestal vase is on the State Dining Room mantel filled with pink and red tulips for a dinner in April 1982 commemorating the three-hundredth anniversary of trade relations between the United States and the Netherlands. Sèvres china was first commissioned in Vincennes, France, in 1756 by Madame de Pompadour and is known for its gold-touched panels of delicate pastorals and birds of gorgeous plumage. (For instructions on re-creating this arrangement, see page 84.)

ABOVE LEFT: *The fireplace in the State Dining Room features cascading arrangements in tall vermeil vases on either side of the Lincoln portrait. They were created in a joint effort with David Jones, who had been Nancy Reagan's florist when she lived in California. The arrangement consists of long, sweeping branches of Russian olive, grasses, tulips, euphorbia, and, as focal points, huge heads of green and white flowering kale. The garlands on the surface of the fireplace are of string smilax accented with clusters of stephanotis.*

ABOVE RIGHT: *A graceful cherry tree is planted and forced to open in the main entrance hall of the White House. The base is a French tub constructed by the carpentry staff and overplanted with ivy, hyacinths, daffodils, and caladium.*

In the late 1890s potted greenery meant luxury. The vogue for potted ferns and flowers dating from Grover Cleveland's time strained the timbers of the White House so severely by William McKinley's term that army engineers had to prop up the East Room floor with stout posts before gala evenings.

The material from which formal containers are made is an important consideration. Silver, vermeil, or silver gilt, and fine porcelain are all used in formal reception rooms at the White House. Vases such as the urn-shaped Sèvres porcelain vase on the State Dining Room mantelpiece (see opposite page) are of a classic shape that will always look stately wherever they are placed. Especially for State Visits, the floral theme was usually extended throughout the Mansion, complementing tabletop displays, sometimes with surprising results. One time, during Cherry Blossom Week in Washington, the National Park Service had to force the blooming of 7- to 8-foot trees that lined the cross hall and foyer. However, the next day it looked as if it had snowed. The floor was covered with small, delicate petals from the cherry blossoms—yet they had done their job so beautifully the night before.

Historically, the uniqueness of Chinese export bowls made them a favorite of presidents and First Ladies for display in formal settings such as Diplomatic Reception Rooms or merely as decorating accents on a pier table for daily enjoyment. Many of these White House bowls are from the late eighteenth century and depict colorful Chinese scenes.

The vermeil bamboo-style bowls from the Kennedy administration are very often used as centerpieces at the White House for State Dinners because their size and height are of the right proportion for visibility and the tablesetting placements around them. Mrs. Kennedy favored filling them with fragrant flowers and fruits to combat the smell of smoking, which was a common after-dinner practice. I often called an impressive soup tureen or wine cooler into service as a formal container in a formal setting. If you want to make this type of arrangement, the flowers can be of any style as long as you expose the uniqueness of the atypical vase. At the White House, such a floral arrangement is usually seasonal and is placed on the pier tables in the main cross hall, which runs between the State Dining Room and the East Room, where after-dinner entertainment follows an elegant meal. Similar arrangements are frequently used on the four matching mantels in the East Room.

ABOVE: *President Gerald Ford converses with Prime Minister Liam Cosgrave of Ireland in the Yellow Oval Room prior to a State Dinner in his honor. The very colorful yet sophisticated pedestal bowl arrangement features irises and snapdragons.*

LEFT: *This container is one of about twenty-five that were fashioned by Tiffany & Company for the Kennedy administration. Approximately twelve inches in diameter and five inches deep, they are made of vermeil—gold-covered sterling silver—with a bamboo pattern. The container is on a beveled mirror to multiply the blooms' reflection. This sample arrangement was made for Nancy Reagan to approve for a future State Dinner. I used cut amaryllis in peach and terra-cotta shades with Icelandic poppies in similar tones, then accented them with blush ixia, white allium, and plum blossoms. This arrangement is very tall when measured from the base to the tip of the blossom branches, approximately 24 to 28 inches. The largest flowers are placed so that they do not obstruct the vision of any guest through the arrangement and therefore facilitate conversation around the table.*

ABOVE: *Lady Bird Johnson stands in front of a White House Coromandel screen. These stunning wooden lacquered screens with intricate gold engravings were produced in China during the seventeenth and eighteenth centuries. The tall, heavily embossed vermeil vase is filled with a loosely packed arrangement of carnations, chrysanthemums, and snapdragons. Jacqueline Kennedy, being fond of things French, had the flower shop adopt this style during the latter part of her tenure.*

The particular taste of each First Lady is always important to White House floral art. Even the cherished Monroe plateau has had its troubled times. Julia Grant, who took a great interest in flower arranging, disliked the plateau for being too simple and old-fashioned. Taking copper wire, she devised a way of decorating it with arches stuffed with flowers. This suited her—for a while. When she then banished the plateau from the dining room, she kept an eye out for something better and found it at last at the Centennial Exposition of 1876 in Philadelphia: a silver image of Longfellow's immortal Hiawatha rowing his canoe over a mirrored Gitchie-Goomie. Julia Grant considered this the paragon of beauty and art for the White House and lovingly garlanded it in white orchids, roses, and camellias. After she left, Hiawatha sailed from the White House table and today is used only occasionally.

RIGHT: *This delicate yet richly hued antique Chinese export bowl was used on a side table in the Diplomatic Reception Room during a visit from President Félix Houphouët-Boigny of the Ivory Coast in May 1962. The flowers are arranged very casually and consist of pale pink tulips and red parrot tulips with white feverfew. The colors of the flowers were often chosen to enhance the paintings that hung above them. The tulips were discouraged from continuing to grow and curve by making a small knife slit under each head.*

Lucy Webb Hayes, a botanist, influenced a dinner for the Russian Grand Dukes Constantine and Alexis. The State Dining Room table was set with an oval mirror representing a lake with tropical banks of ferns and trailing vines. In the center of the lake was a hill formed with vases of tropical fruit and scattered columns of candied fruits and bonbons. Delicate pink and white vases of frosted glass and silver strands stood at each plate, holding pink and white buds. Azalea trees and other flowering plants were arranged about the room, ornamenting the chocolate and strawberry pyramids that stood at the north side of the room. String smilax on gilt wires was draped about the table, in the chandeliers, and over pictures.

TOP LEFT: *Mrs. Clinton reviews an early-summer sample table setting of creamy white roses and Queen Anne's lace with Nancy Clarke.*

BOTTOM LEFT: *The subtle colors of white calla lilies and pink roses are stylishly offset by the dark tablecloth in a centerpiece for a State Dinner honoring President Ali Abdullah Saleh of Yemen given by President and Mrs. Bush in January 1991. It's a look of pure elegance.*

LEFT: *This pair of vermeil champagne buckets flanking the French clock in the foyer were filled with branches of forced cherry blossoms, peach and orange poppies, and a small white allium.*

Developing a successful floral design for a formal event means more than selecting the right containers and flowers; it involves creating an atmosphere that will contribute to the enjoyment of all the guests. At a dinner held by President and Mrs. Reagan in August 1981 for President and Mrs. Anwar Sadat of Egypt, the tables were dressed in coral silk moiré cloths with vermeil bowls holding coral, ivory, and pale yellow roses. In a *Washington Post* article the following day, Elisabeth Bumiller wrote, "The perfumes and smell of the flowers, mixed with the low lights, gave the women milky complexions for at least one night. 'Everything's so soigné,' said an utterly serious C. Z. Guest, the New York socialite. 'All the flowers, the plants, the perfect taste.'"

RIGHT: *The textures—frilly and velvety—as well as the pretty colors and fragrances of white peonies and pink roses welcome guests for a State Dinner honoring President Kim Dae Jung of South Korea hosted by President and Mrs. Clinton.*

RIGHT: *In the relatively low lighting under this outdoor tent where First Lady Hillary Clinton joins guests for the Friends of Art Dinner, the contrast of vibrant red and white flowers seems to light up the tables.*

Step-by-Step
INTRODUCTION

a hobby such as flower arranging is the joyous task of finding beautiful and unusual containers for holding your flowers. Silver of all kinds, pedestal bonbons, cut glass bowls, and lovely antique or reproduction pieces of Chinese export ware look lovely in a more formal Federal setting among highly polished woods, velvets, and silk brocades. If you are fortunate enough to own family heirloom pieces, take them out of the closet and bring them to life with fresh flowers. Today with the emphasis on more classical home decor, you can even obtain authentic White House reproduction bowls and vases in various shapes and materials.

You may also discover beautiful, unique containers at flea markets, consignment shops, and antique dealers. The insides of priceless antiques, such as the ones I used at the White House, must be treated with care so as not to blemish the surface with floral residue or preservative. Although I had the luxury of having custom-fit liners made by the metal shop in the White House basement, I find that different kinds of ice cream containers, margarine tubs, and tuna fish cans make satisfactory liners for my most valuable, personal vases.

At the White House, I often used professional florist's techniques to obtain the perfect floral arrangement. For a precious-metal footed compote container that held grapes and other fruit in addition to flowers, I pushed a potato onto a pin holder and wired the grapes to a floral pick, which I then inserted into the potato. To secure long-stemmed blooms, I crisscrossed clear floral tape over the top of a vase to create an invisible mesh support system. Also, a flimsy stem can be made more rigid by placing it into a clear straw before inserting it into the arrangement. 🖋

FAMILLE ROSE BOWL— RHAPSODY IN FLOWERS

Plastic dishpan filled with foam to fit the bowl
2 stems of amaryllis "apple blossom"
18 pale pink kyria roses
12 terra cotta leonidas roses
12 deep terra-cotta-colored mini calla lilies
1 bunch of lady's mantle
Bamboo stake
Moss

1. Place the dishpan inside the bowl and put fresh green moss around the outer edges.

2. Take one stem of amaryllis and put a bamboo stake into the stem, fill with water, and plug the bottom with cotton or a wad of tissue.

3. Make a hole in the foam just large enough for the stem to be pushed in, keeping the height of the stem about one and a half to two times the width of the bowl. Cut the other amaryllis stem and proceed as with the first one, keeping the height of the head of the blossom just below the first one.

4. Next add the pale pink kyria roses, then the terra-cotta-colored roses and the calla lilies. Keep moving the bowl around so that your arrangement is nicely rounded with a fairly even color mix.

5. Finally, add the lady's mantle. Its soft lime green color will really set off the colors of the roses and the calla lilies.

METAL URN FOR A FOYER

6 tuberoses

4 hydrangeas

1 agapanthus

4 leonidas roses

4 "Autumn Joy" sedums

6 purple-and-white-variegated
*   lisianthus*

3 monbretia

5 "Crispa" nerines

5 veronicas

1 head of flowering kale

2 artichokes

Floral foam

Sheet moss

1. Fill a large urn with foam and cover with sheet moss. Note: be sure to test the metal container to be certain that it is watertight; some are not.

2. Start by placing the six tuberoses in the urn to establish the size. The flowers in this type of container may be arranged in an exaggerated fashion, so the tallest flower may be at least two and a half times the height of the urn.

3. Next add the hydrangeas to give weight to your arrangement.

4. Continue with the agapanthus in the center and fill in with the remaining roses, the sedums, the lisianthus, and then the monbretia, nerines, and veronicas. These last slender flowers give the arrangement an airy look.

5. Insert the kale in low, front and center as a focal point, and add the artichokes for interest.

HAND-BLOWN DEEP GLASS BOWL

When creating this display, make sure that the arrangement has a loose, airy look in keeping with the sparkling clear container. Space is as important a component in this type of arrangement as the flowers.

6 leonidas roses
8 to 9 stems of yellow oncidium orchids
Handful of bear grass
Small floral foam
Posy clay

1. Soak the floral foam in water containing preservative and anchor to the base of the bowl with posy clay.

2. Cut the three most open roses very short and place in the foam, covering it as much as possible.

3. Place one rose about 14 inches tall in the center of the foam, a second, about 11 to 12 inches tall, out to the right, and the third, slightly taller than the edge of the container, in approximately a parallel line from the first.

4. After washing the bear grass to remove any soil and dirt, cut off all of the white part of the stem. Holding the stems in one hand and grasping the other end of the bunch with your other hand, swirl it into a circle and place inside the bowl, manipulating it as necessary to further hide the foam.

5. Keeping the first two stems of the oncidium long, angle them out to the right side, keeping them as horizontal as possible. Place two or three more upright to the left of the roses, and fill in as needed with the rest.

Four-Bowl
Iron Epergne

If you do not have an epergne, a multiarmed candelabra may be used by placing an adapter or holder made of silver, glass, or plastic into the candle cup and adding foam and flowers.

4 large hydrangea heads
5 pink nerines
8 light pink Melani roses
4 chincherinchees
4 white nerines
11 purple veronicas
7 stems of white freesia
Several sprigs of ivy
4 bunches of grapes
Floral foam
Floral tape

1. Fill four small bowls in the epergne with water-soaked foam and tape down securely.

2. Place a short-stemmed hydrangea head into each bowl, fitting it snugly into the foam.

3. Cut the stems of all of the flowers to 3 to 6 inches long.

4. Add a mix of the flowers by placing the stems through the hydrangea blossom, with some very close to the head of the flower and some extending outward for interest.

5. Complete the arrangement by adding sprigs of ivy, then the grapes, leaving some hanging over the edge of each small bowl.

Historic how-to

FRENCH TULIPS

*Large pedestal container
    (if valuable, use a liner)
36 red and pink tulips*

*Floral foam
Flower preservative*

1. Soak the floral foam in water and flower preservative.

2. Place the foam into the liner and the liner into the container.

3. Several hours or a day before arranging, cut the tulip stems, preferably under water. About half of the tulips should be wrapped in wax paper and then wet newspaper, and placed in a deep container with preservative. This will keep the stems straight. The remainder should be put into a shorter container to allow their heads to bend over the sides of the bucket.

4. Place the tallest, straightest tulips at the center of the arrangement. Next, arrange the rest of the tulips around the outside to form a "frame." Continue filling in with the straight and curved tulips, making sure that many tulip heads extend downward over the sides of the vase.

*Detail of photograph
on page 68*

Historic how-to

ELEGANT DAISIES

*12-to-18-inch-round container,
   3 to 5 inches deep
33 gerbera daisies
Several stems of fern or other greenery*

*Floral anchor tape
2 blocks of floral foam soaked in
   water with preservative*

1. Place a block of floral foam into the container, having it extend above the top of the container by 1 inch. Wedge pieces of floral foam on each side to secure. Place a crisscross of floral tape over the top of the container to assist in keeping the flower heads straight and in place.

2. Place the daisies into the foam varying the stems in length from 10 to 20 inches long, making sure the ends are stuck into the foam as deep as possible. At least 1 ½ to 2 inches of the stem should be in the foam. (To condition the gerbera, cut the stems under water and place into a tall container of lukewarm water and preservative.)

3. Fill in with the greenery to cover the foam.

4. Keeping the arrangement misted daily and the water level high will promote longevity.

*Detail of photograph
on page 66*

INFORMAL AND WHIMSICAL CONTAINERS

During Lady Bird Johnson's live television tour of the White House grounds in 1965, she declared that fresh flowers in any room "give a feeling of welcome, of expectancy." She was particularly fond of informal arrangements with seasonal flowers in straw baskets as the perfect touch to say, "This room is ready for enjoyment." Her love of spring and summer flowers, a favorite being peonies—and of course Texas wildflowers—strongly influenced her Beautification campaign. She worked very hard to encourage roadside plantings, first around Washington and then the entire country. So I was delighted to create my very first centerpiece in the Executive Mansion for Mrs. Ford with the china bowls from the service chosen by Mrs. Johnson during her husband's administration.

ABOVE LEFT: *First Lady Betty Ford and Happy Rockefeller, wife of Vice President Nelson Rockefeller, share a light lunch in the solarium. The cheery addition to their table is a pretty silver bowl bursting with deep blue delphiniums, white carnations, and yellow pompoms and chrysanthemums.*

ABOVE RIGHT: *Jacqueline Kennedy loved using baskets to hold her floral bouquets. In 1962, she gave a luncheon for senators' wives in the State Dining Room and decorated the tables with gold-painted baskets filled in her signature uncontrived fashion with lilies, baby's breath, tulips, irises, and marguerites.*

ABOVE: *Every spring, the First Lady holds a luncheon for senators' wives. Here is a close-up of a centerpiece for a luncheon hosted by Barbara Bush: one in a series of playful stuffed toys is nestled in roses, peonies, lilies, nerines, and sweet peas.*

When Betty Ford assumed her responsibility as First Lady, her move was not planned. The country was preparing for the Bicentennial, and there was a great deal of expectancy and excitement. A less resourceful woman might have panicked, but Mrs. Ford took command graciously and set out to make her administration a memorable one. As her first social secretary, she hired Nancy Ruwe from the State Department, who knew just about everything in matters of entertaining protocol. Mrs. Ford was very innovative in her ideas about tablescapes, and many formal affairs such as State Dinners were decorated with decidedly informal centerpieces. She liked seeing her favorite orange lilies, Fuji chrysanthemums, and gerbera daisies loosely arranged, "so they can breathe."

The Johnson china service in which I made my inaugural arrangement features a delicate border of various state wildflowers on a pristine off-white background. The bowls are 12 inches in diameter and decorated with a motif of Texas wildflowers. Mrs. Ford, along with her social secretary, Maria Downs, who succeeded Nancy Ruwe, had decided to use these for an athlete's prayer breakfast in February 1975.

Once we had established the color scheme for the flowers and table linens, our staff set to work on filling the bowls with yellow marguerites, pompoms, blue delphinium, and bachelor's buttons, with accents of pussy willow. On top of the pale yellow tablecloths, the bouquets of early spring blooms brightened a rather gray winter's day. I can still vividly recall my thrill when I opened my invitation to attend that same breakfast!

Probably Mrs. Ford's most outstanding contribution to interior design at the White House was her display of American craft artifacts. She showcased handmade objects such as antique weathervanes and wheel-thrown pottery throughout the Executive Mansion. Even dinner tables were often covered with quilts from Appalachia. At a dinner for Prime Minister Harold Wilson of Great Britain, an amateur ornithologist, the tables were decorated with a collection of antique bird decoys; bronze horse sculptures were used at a dinner for Prime Minister Liam Cosgrave of Ireland; folk art animals delighted guests at an annual governors' dinner; and antique pan scales for the federal judiciary.

One of my favorite centerpieces inspired by an everyday object was for a Senate Ladies' Luncheon hosted by Nancy Reagan. At a millinery supplier, I found some floppy straw garden hats reminiscent of a Victorian tea party. I turned each hat upside down and placed a one-gallon ice cream container inside. We then filled each container with a lush cluster of peach florabunda roses and tied the whole frothy floral mass together with soft green velvet ribbon. Each guest was always presented with a keepsake gift at her place setting, and that year everyone was given a pale peach, miniature rose made of porcelain.

ABOVE: *These upside-down straw garden hat centerpieces, brimming with peach-colored floribunda roses, complement the Johnson china service perfectly at Nancy Reagan's Senate Ladies' Luncheon.*

BELOW: *This garden hat filled with flowers was a real conversation piece! In the background, one guest seems to have brought her own!*

In choosing new official White House china, Lady Bird Johnson employed a Napoleonic eagle center design from President Monroe's china service with wildflowers from all fifty states and the District of Columbia, forty different patterns in all. The service was made by Tiffany & Co., and the dessert plates were hand-painted. Mrs. Johnson's interest in conservation and beautification was well known. Large and small bowls made for serving and for flower arrangements were ordered and first used at the Senate Ladies' Luncheon in May 1968, filled with bouquets of spring flowers on round tables with pale yellow cloths under organdy covers.

Edith Roosevelt liked her arrangements to seem natural, as though she had walked in the garden and plucked the blossoms herself, then placed them in the vase, with no stringent effort to suggest formal art. Early in Theodore Roosevelt's administration, the White House underwent a major remodeling that preserved and enhanced its historical character and connection to George Washington, while introducing new spaces and modern conveniences. The architects urged the demolition of the conservatories that were attached to the western side. Mrs. Roosevelt hesitated for a long time and then yielded at last, for historical reasons. She never ceased missing them and later planted what she called her "colonial garden" on part of their site, where she gathered old-fashioned flowers in the spring, summer, and fall.

LEFT: *These "mini-gardens in a bag" centerpieces were an essential part of one outdoor event on the grounds of the White House. They were created for First Lady Betty Ford's hosting of the Brown Bag Picnic Lunch for Republican congressional wives on a gorgeous June day in 1975. Each bag contained a plastic liner in which were "planted" red carnations, feverfew, and bachelor's buttons.*

Nearly every President and First Lady at some time choose to entertain on the south grounds of the White House, especially in the summer months. Frequently these are large social events such as clambakes, barbecues, and picnics, where guests are seated at long wooden tables covered with red-and-white-checked cloths. For these affairs, I have made floral displays using baskets, mason jars, terra-cotta planters, and even rolled-down paper bags holding plastic containers brimming with garden flowers such as zinnias and geraniums that can withstand the extreme Washington heat.

The Carter family enjoyed that type of entertaining, usually with a great many people in attendance. Rosalynn Carter appointed Gretchen Poston, a partner in a party-planning business in Washington, to be her social secretary. Since the Carters were not Washington insiders, Gretchen was invaluable to them; she knew the best local sources for all the things necessary to put on a successful event. Her ideas for new and clever table themes were aimed at creating amusing diversions for the seated guests. Art objects mixed with flowers are, thankfully, apolitical and offer a topic of conversation that is noncontroversial.

Having been a guest at White House luncheons and dinners, I know how grateful one can be for someone at the table to break the ice with a remark about the music or centerpieces. For one event, Gretchen received dozens of flowered sheets as a donation. In addition to our flo-

LEFT: *This lovely portrait of Rosalynn Carter, in front of a Monet painting, includes a beautiful Chinese export bowl that is holding a tight arrangement in the Williamsburg style of fall-color flowers. There are yellows, oranges, and lavenders, consisting of gerberas, delphiniums, and chrysanthemums.*

ral arrangement, our flower shop staff was given the task of cutting the sheets up to use as napkins and as linings for the guests' picnic basket lunches. It was a beautifully coordinated theme.

A very whimsical container that was a challenge to work with was a real cowboy boot. The request came straight from the Chief Executive, who was fond of horseback riding on his ranch in California. President Reagan was hosting a barbecue for the Professional Rodeo Cowboys Association, and we needed about six or seven dozen pairs of boots to serve as flower holders. Our request was sent to a Texas bootmaker.

The bootmaker granted our request to borrow these 70 or 80 boots, but the shipment had an unusual twist; we opened the boxes to find absolutely exquisite boots with vibrantly colored snakeskin and alligator—all for the left foot! I suppose the bootmaker was ensuring that no one would walk away with a pair of centerpieces. I quickly focused on designing the strategy to hold the flowers inside the boots as well as the boots on the table. First we tried placing a brick in the leg to weigh it down, with a container filled with bright zinnias, strands of bittersweet, and fall leaves spilling from the top, but a test run showed us that a brisk breeze would knock the boots over.

So it was back to the drawing board, this time with the help of the White House carpenters. We came up with the idea of anchoring the boots with cleats to blocks of wood cut about an inch and a half longer than the sole of each boot. Before the boots were fitted to the blocks, we covered the blocks with the same red-and-white gingham tablecloth material we were using on the picnic tables. We had to work fast, but the finished product was a centerpiece that wasn't going to go anywhere, even in a gusty wind.

Weather conditions were always a concern when planning an outdoor event, and we all needed to be able to cope with unpredicted changes. If, at the last minute, rain moved an event inside, I simply added lots of candles to illuminate the flowers, especially if they were of a deep hue. For another Reagan barbecue on the South Lawn for five hundred congressional delegates and their families, Mrs. Reagan and I had selected brilliant red cut-geranium centerpieces on blue-and-white-checked tablecloths. Two days before the event, we were informed that the cloths would not be ready in time, and we had to substitute large red bandannas instead. I added some natural wheat and yellow daisies to the arrangements, and no one would ever have imagined that an entertaining crisis had taken place.

This unique cowboy boot floral display was a big hit with the President and all of his professional cowboy guests, too.

One of the great advantages of the old conservatories, which stood from 1856 to 1902, were that they produced the flowers for a prodigious number of gift bouquets. It had long been a tradition for the First Lady to call upon people of importance when they visited Washington. The sheer numbers of visitors turned this tradition into an ordeal. Eventually the coachman would take a calling card to the person's house when it was fairly clear that the person would not be at home. Then the guest would be invited to a large tea or similar gathering. Mrs. Grant conceived the idea of sending bouquets with the card. What a hit this was! Printed cards soon developed, and the arrangements, taken by the coachman, were delivered with directions on how to transfer them to vases. At the time the conservatories were demolished, the White House employed five full-time "bouquet makers." The elegant custom was replaced by an increased program of large teas and musicals during winter and garden parties in spring. And the shortcut provided by the telephone changed many such complicated customs with time.

Sunny yellow has been a popular color choice of many First Ladies. In an interview with *Ladies' Home Journal* in 1960, Pat Nixon called yellow "her favorite morning color" and she frequently requested yellow daisies on her table as her most prized flowers. She also began the trend of incorporating unusual items like driftwood in centerpieces. I share her fond memories about her love for flowers of all types: "I have always loved to garden, you know a riot of color, flowers of all kinds. I loved sprinkling that garden, still love to water flowers—the dust disappears, the leaves turn green again, and the fragrance is so wonderful, so fresh." Pat Nixon was responsible for inaugurating the spring Rose Garden tours at the White House. This has proven over the years to be one of the best attended public exhibitions of the historic grounds.

It was not just the First Ladies who had flower preferences. President Jimmy Carter enjoyed seeing a porcelain bowl filled with fresh flowers in the Oval Office when he arrived for work at 6:30 in the morning. It was also common for Chief White House Floral Decorator Rusty Young to create informal arrangements for gatherings predominantly of men, such as Cabinet meetings and congressional breakfasts. Three silver chop bowls flanked by Revere bowls were often placed on the bare meeting table, sporting seasonal blooms such as delphiniums, plumed celosia, baby's breath, roses, bachelor's buttons, and Peruvian lilies in white or yellow. President Kennedy always wore a blue cornflower in his lapel for formal dinners. But Presidents are not always so easily pleased. Once, at a State Dinner, President Lyndon Johnson picked up the centerpiece and had it removed from the room because it contained lilies of the valley and he found the scent too strong. 🖌

OPPOSITE: *This very inviting and sunny table decor was designed by Nancy Clarke for the annual Congressional Picnic hosted by President and Mrs. Bill Clinton in June 1998. The natural baskets overflowing with yellow roses and Queen Anne's lace look radiant in the South Lawn pavilion.*

RIGHT: *At a navy mess table, President Ronald Reagan's placesetting includes a simple low arrangement of heather carnations, snapdragons, and Fuji chrysanthemums, not to mention the requisite jar of jelly beans.*

ABOVE TOP: *A working luncheon is much more pleasant outside, when possible. Here on a terrace near the oval office, President Ronald Reagan and Vice President George Bush discuss matters and share their table with a basket of yellow lilies, pink roses, and white freesia.*

ABOVE BOTTOM: *In the Oval Office, President George Bush and Vice President Dan Quayle have a bite to eat while working. The arrangement in the foreground consists of roses, marguerites, snapdragons, and alstromeria.*

In today's White House most of the flowers are purchased from wholesale florists, but the Victorian White House had a rich resource for flowers in the extensive conservatories linked to the west end of the house, in part where the West Wing now stands. Here orchids, camellias, roses, and many other flowers were available all winter to adorn the White House containers. Presidential families took their leisure in the "glass houses" while snow fell. Grover Cleveland's daughter remembered that the smell of roses pervaded the house. Longtime office staff member Octavius Pruden painted this favorite orchid in watercolors for youthful First Lady Frances Folsom Cleveland, who had admired it in the conservatory.

Step-by-Step

INTRODUCTION

jars, diverse woven baskets, opaque oriental-shaped vases, and every type of metal container, contemporary glassware remains a very popular and subtle choice holder for fresh flowers. A clear, nearly invisible glass vase with a narrow neck will need no extra support for the flower stems. Just make sure that the stem placement is in harmony with the flowers in the arrangement and not bent at angles that detract from the array. If the vase's mouth is too wide, some clear floral tape crisscrossed over the top will position them better.

You may also try using a clear drinking tumbler inside of the container or partially filling the vase with polished stones, sea glass, seashells, cranberries, even lemons or limes. Also, loosely knotted plastic tubing makes an interesting underwater holder for an ultramodern look. If the glass is colored, I use common sand to elevate the liner within the vase before adding flowers. This can also improve the stability of the display and be just the trick needed with a very tall container and shorter-stemmed flowers. And low ceramic dish containers generally require a pin holder secured with posy clay to hold the stems upright.

Adorning a rustic basket with freshly harvested garden flowers may appear effortless, but the best arrangements need a bit of work to make them last. You should insert the stems into a cottage cheese container filled with water-soaked foam. Sometimes I wrap the foam in chicken wire to prevent it from crumbling inside the container. And a little wisely placed Spanish moss pressed over the top of the basket will hide the unsightly mechanics. With informal floral arrangements there really are no steadfast rules, and overcoming the challenges of your container with inspired design will often be almost as pleasurable as admiring your final creation. 🌿

HONG BOWL

When using a valuable container such as this beautiful Hong bowl, always protect the inside of the container with a liner. Plastic dishpans of various sizes are perfect for such bowls.

9 pale pink tulips
9 reddish pink tulips
8 purple/white variegated lisianthus
8 peach roses
8 yellow freesia
3 purple brodeas
Seeded eucalyptus
8 pink rice flowers
Floral tape
Floral foam
Moss

1. Fill the bowl liner with foam, crisscross floral tape over the edges of the dishpan, and cover the edges with moss.

2. Start by placing the tulips fairly evenly throughout the bowl, making sure some curve nicely over the edges of the bowl.

3. Add the lisianthus in the same fashion, then the roses, freesia, and brodeas.

4. Add short pieces of seeded eucalyptus and finish off with pieces of the pink rice flowers. Make sure as you are adding each type of flower that you have some tall ones and some short ones to create more interest and depth.

ANTIQUE LEATHER-HANDLE WOODEN BOX

(All ingredients are preserved)

Liner fitted with dry foam
1 small pheasant feather wreath
2 dried hydrangeas
2 pheasant feather balls
2 pheasant feather stars
2 pomegranates
2 preserved chestnuts
1 cluster of brunia albiflora
2 or 3 pieces of preserved reed grass
2 green amaranthus
Small handful of Spanish moss
6-inch wooden picks

1. Place 6-inch wooden picks into the side of the pheasant feather wreath and insert into the liner at the left side of the handle.

2. Place the hydrangeas to cover the foam in front of the wreath.

3. Next, add the pheasant feather balls and stars on picks into the hydrangeas.

4. Nestle the pomegranates and chestnuts, also wired onto picks, into the box.

5. Finish the look with one stem of the brunia and several stems of reed grass, plus two shorter pieces of amaranthus hanging over the edge of the box.

6. Tuck in Spanish moss to provide accent color and cover any mechanics that might be showing.

BURGUNDY POTTERY JARDINIÈRE

Berries and fruit always add a special, unexpected look to an arrangement.

> *5 large oak-leaf hydrangeas*
> *3 large green calla lilies*
> *2 long stems of red beech*
> *2 stems of palm dates*
> *Floral foam*
> *Bunch of moss*

1. Fill the container with foam, placing moss around the outside edges.

2. Place one hydrangea about twice the height of the container in the center back.

3. Fill the front area with shorter stems of hydrangea, angling some out to the sides.

4. Make three large holes in the foam in the right rear and insert three calla lilies, keeping them slightly taller than the tallest hydrangea.

5. Finish off with the two stems of palm dates in the front, hanging over the edge of the container, and fill in with beech.

PAIR OF DOLPHIN CANDLESTICKS

2 mini eggplants
3 to 4 baby zucchini
2 pieces of ginger
4 tomatillos
5 baby red potatoes
6 white onions
6 to 7 red crab apples
4 shallots
3 stems of salmon-colored
*   floribunda roses*
6 stems of ivy
2 stems of St. John's wort
Reindeer moss
2 pieces of floral foam

1. Anchor the floral foam to the top of the candlesticks with tape.

2. Using short picks, first attach the small eggplant to the cage. Then turn the stick around, and add the zucchini and the piece of ginger.

3. Continue to add half of the vegetables to each cage with picks: 2 tomatillos, 2 red potatoes, 3 onions, and 2 shallots.

4. Cut the stems of the floribunda roses very short and add half of them to each cage. Stick these in separately between the vegetables.

5. Place the stem ends of the ivy into the floral foam and push the tendrils gently in between the flowers and vegetables.

6. Complete the look by adding short clusters of St. John's wort and reindeer moss where they are needed.

GREENHOUSE WITH SUNFLOWERS

The finished arrangement should look as if it were gathered and placed randomly in the pail.

Plastic liner
Galvanized aluminum pail
10 sunflowers
4 hydrangeas
7 orange/red cockscombs
5 "Orange Flame" celosia
6 "Autumn Joy" sedums
3 ornamental yellow peppers
1 red chili pepper
Floral foam
Moss

1. Place a foam-filled plastic liner in an old galvanized pail. Stuff in moss to hide the edges.

2. Place the sunflowers in the foam, keeping them spread evenly throughout the pail and at varying heights.

3. Add the hydrangeas to fill in the spaces among the sunflowers.

4. Add the cockscombs, celosia, sedums, ornamental peppers, and chili pepper in a casual fashion.

For this Annual Governors of States and Territories Dinner, each Native American porcelain figure situated on the miniature landscape centerpieces represented a different territory of the continental United States. Each state governor was seated at a table with the corresponding tribal figurine and the flowers and plant material that were indigenous to the Native American's home territory.

GOVERNORS' DINNER INDIAN SCULPTURE CENTERPIECE

Each year the President and First Lady hold a formal dinner for the state governors and their wives. I wanted to create something truly American, so I decided to use magnificent porcelain Indian figurines. We borrowed them for this occasion. They are modeled after each of the many Native American tribes from across the country.

1 glass quiche dish, 12 to 14 inches in diameter	Small pots of primrose or English daisies
Porcelain or china figurine	Mini African violets
Cut fern	Floral foam
Cut ivy	Small rocks and pebbles
2 to 3 narcissus	Moss
Flowering branch material such as apple, cherry, or forsythia	Votive candles

1. Soak the foam in water with preservative and then place in the glass dish. A small iron or pottery bonsai container or low terra-cotta planter may also be used. If you are using a container with a drainage hole, be sure to have a saucer to match.

2. Cover foam with fresh green moss to approximate a living landscape; spray with water.

3. Place figure securely on the moss.

4. Insert the sprigs of fern, ivy, narcissus, and flowering branches to imitate tufts of shrubs. Position some rocks and pebbles artistically over the landscape.

5. For the final touch, place a few small pots of flowers on the moss. This richly textured arrangement is perfect for a special luncheon. At night, add a few votive candles to light up this little piece of the planet.

5

UPSTAIRS IN THE FAMILY QUARTERS

Much of the White House, especially the State and Diplomatic floors, remains relatively unchanged as a museum of American and European furnishings and art from administration to administration. However, upstairs in the Family Quarters, on the second and third floors of the White House known as the Residence, the carpeting, furniture, heirlooms, personal belongings, and, on occasion, even the wall coverings are replaced by each First Family who moves in to live there. When friends and acquaintances of the President and First Lady send flowers from local florists as gifts, they are always directed to the flower shop so as to be placed upstairs wherever the colors would be best suited. President Gerald Ford loved proteas in his Residence office after being introduced to them at a friend's house and later receiving them as a gift.

Mamie Eisenhower was very fond of gladioli. The mantels were often decorated with large fan-shaped bouquets of yellow gladioli.

In contrast, Jacqueline Kennedy did not want flowers to be placed on the mantels, as had been the custom for decades. She requested her floral staff to place arrangements only against the north walls of rooms and on circular tables, such as in the center of the Blue Room. Mrs. Kennedy also replaced the use of clear glass vases with vermeil and chinese export bowls.

Floral themes have always been popular in First Ladies' private rooms. When Mrs. Kennedy renovated the White House, she papered her dressing room with French wallpaper decorated with delicate blue flowers and birds. Later Mrs. Johnson adorned her bedroom with a bedspread of soft gold, coral, and green flowers. These are the rooms where the First Ladies truly enjoy the fragrance and touch of natural beauty afforded by fresh flowers. Our flower shop staff always placed arrangements in the second-floor cross hall, the Yellow Oval Room, the West Sitting Room, the Family Dining Room, the President's and First Lady's bedrooms, the President's office, and the First Lady's dressing room. The flowers for offices were simple bouquets or potted plants such as African violets, made to fit on desks or credenzas. Very often they were created by using recycled flowers from large State Dinner displays or decorations from the Blue, Red, or Green rooms.

When State Visits occurred, the foreign guests and dignitaries would usually stay at Blair House, the State Department guest house across the street from 1600 Pennsylvania Avenue. On the evening of the State Dinner, they would be transported via limousine to the North Portico. Then they would ascend the grand staircase to the Residence for a short reception in the Yellow Oval Room, where official gifts would sometimes be exchanged.

After that period, the President and First Lady and their guests would descend the stairs and enter the dining room. In the Yellow Sit-

President and Mrs. Gerald Ford entertain Queen Elizabeth II of England and Prince Philip in the President's Dining Room during the Bicentennial celebration in 1976, using the Society of the Cincinnati service. These plates, part of President George Washington's personal china, were commissioned for officers who served in the American Revolution and purchased for Washington by General Henry Lee in 1786.

ting Room, I often kept small vases of stars of Bethlehem among the objets d'art on the mantelpiece and grander, more elegant arrangements of melon-hued gerbera on side tables. The entrance to the sitting room is flanked by mahogany pedestals upon which I placed tobacco leaf reproduction cachepots, usually holding a Boston fern or other plant. But for a State Visit the same pots would be filled with huge bouquets of lilies and roses, gerbera, and possibly sweet-smelling stock. These events required the most impeccable floral designs to compliment the upstairs private quarters with the more elaborate arrangements for the public venues and dinner tables.

My very favorite look in this area, however, came for a while in the fall, when I would go out to the National Arboretum and have one of the groundsmen cut long branches of all different varieties of crab apples. Although there are no longer any actual growing greenhouses on the White House premises, the National Park Service, under the guidance of Irv Williams, provided our White House flower shop with small flowering plants, which we used in several areas of the Residence and State Floor. These were kept in a small holding house on the roof. The large ficus and palm trees for display in the Executive Mansion were cared for and maintained in tip-top condition by the Park Service in greenhouses outside Washington. After taking the crab apple branches back to the shop, we would strip them of all of their foliage, leaving only the brightly colored crab apples in all sizes and shades, from the deepest red to the palest yellow.

ABOVE TOP: *A custom of foreign dignitaries visiting the President and First Lady is to sign the guest book in the main hall of the Residence. Here Prime Minister Margaret Thatcher and her husband, Denis, are welcomed by President and Mrs. Ronald Reagan. A spectacular arrangement of all-white lilies, snapdragons, French tulips, and carnations enlivens the table.*

ABOVE BOTTOM: *President and Mrs. Ronald Reagan talk for a few minutes in the upstairs Yellow Oval Room before greeting their guests for a State Dinner in honor of the President of Mexico. A pretty arrangement of pink spray roses adds just the right hint of color to this subtly hued sitting room.*

BELOW: *At a working luncheon between President George Bush and Prime Minister Anand Panyarachun of Thailand, the polished wooden table is decorated with three bowls of deep red and pale pink roses in a very simple but elegant round shape.*

Upstairs in the Family Quarters **111**

LEFT: *The President's Dining Room can be the setting for formal dinners as well as informal family meals. Here President Ronald Reagan is toasting Crown Prince Akihito of Japan at a dinner party during his visit to the United States in 1987. The grand centerpieces are tall topiaries made of greens and white roses.*

BOTTOM LEFT: *President and Mrs. George Bush entertain President and Mrs. Boris Yeltsin of the U.S.S.R. with the help of the Bushes' dog Millie, who is relaxing on the floor. Their intimate luncheon table is decorated with pale pink roses, copper-colored floribunda roses, lilies, and snapdragons.*

OPPOSITE TOP: *This is a sample tablescape created for a Reagan State Dinner. Our flower shop crew worked for several weeks designing the topiary forms of chicken wire and mosses. We created every sort of animal shape, then covered them with ivy and creeping fig. They were then anchored to a base of moss in a waterproof clay saucer. Cut amaryllis, white allium, and white Scotch broom were added to complete the environment.*

Sometimes a foreign leader makes an unofficial visit to the United States and a formal dinner is held in the President's or Family Dining Room on the second floor. This room can accommodate three or four tables of eight seatings each and is a magnificent setting with its historic wallpaper and marble mantelpieces. The round tables are usually covered with cloths of pale peach or yellow with lace overlays, and the Tiffany bamboo vermeil bowls are filled with ivory tulips, freesia, and pale peach lilies accented with strands of ivy to create a stunningly simple statement under the flattering light of multiple candles, some as tall as 24 to 30 inches.

Floral motifs have been enhancing White House entertaining since the nineteenth century. First Lady Sarah Polk ordered the first official White House china service in 1846. The fruit baskets and compotes are each adorned with a different, beautiful flower; the 9-inch dessert plates have a wide apple green border with a patriotic shield, and each bears a unique, grand flower in its off-white center. In 1870, Julia Grant obtained 587 pieces of china adorned with coats of arms and a wide array of hand-painted flowers, including orange field lily, Virginia creeper, lilac, and wild rose. Like the Polk service, the plates are edged in gold and were made in the porcelain factories of France. The magnificent Hayes china, inspired by First Lady Lucy Webb Hayes in 1880, boasts unusual unique interpretations of American flora and fauna, has a ten-sided angular soup bowl that conforms to the contours of the mountain laurel flower, and has a cluster of these flowers as its principal design.

Lady Bird Johnson enjoys a quiet moment upstairs in the Lincoln Sitting Room with a small pierced vermeil bowl and tray filled with pink snapdragons and red, pink, and white miniature carnations in a simple all-around arrangement.

resident Abraham Lincoln kept his office upstairs, in a room that is now named for him and is the principal White House guest room. The ornate carved rosewood bed was purchased by Mrs. Lincoln in 1860 for the State Guest Room, then known as the Prince of Wales Room after the first royalty to ever sleep in the White House. Before it was a guest room, this room probably saw few, if any flowers, unless they were pinned to Lincoln's secretaries, John Nicolay and John Hay, when they went upstairs to bed after a State Dinner. As a guest room, it is amply supplied with handsome arrangements, often of spring flowers in antique vases, and the idea is carried through to the adjacent Lincoln Sitting Room.

Mrs. Kennedy had a kitchen installed in the Residence so she could feed her children, and it has been a very welcome addition ever since. Most evenings, the First Family has a casual meal in the dining room, served on place mats on the mahogany table. I always kept a bowl of fresh seasonal flowers in the center so that the table was always ready whenever the First Family needed it. When the President and First Lady had personal houseguests, their rooms were also on our list for flowers. They would occupy a couple of the gracious guest rooms, such as the Queen's Room, which at the time was decorated in very soft pastel ivory, melon, and peach shades. On the bedside tables, I would place vermeil beakers filled with delicate clusters of miniature roses and stars of Bethlehem, or, in the spring, lovely arching vases of peach tulips. The Lincoln Bedroom and Sitting Room, where President Nixon kept a fire burning year-round and where he liked to smoke cigars, was decorated in a more masculine fashion with bowls of red roses or bright yellow tulips.

Around a charming floral centerpiece of roses, snapdragons, and red hot poker, Rosalynn Carter shares a meal with family members in November 1979.

ABOVE LEFT: *First Lady Rosalynn Carter sits at the desk in her study in the Residence with a gift from her husband, a long-stemmed red rose.*

ABOVE RIGHT: *First Lady Rosalynn Carter and Joan Mondale, wife of Vice President Fritz Mondale, have tea in the solarium, Mrs. Carter's favorite room in the White House. The casually stylish bouquet of yellow roses, blue iris and delphinium, miniature carnations, and yellow and white daisies looks crisp and summery on the glass tabletop.*

Rosalynn Carter loved flowers in the Residence. She was very partial to roses. When she and Jimmy lived in the Governor's Mansion in Georgia, there was a lovely rose garden on the grounds, so she often requested arrangements of just-picked stems throughout the house. It was a great pleasure to her to have the Rose Garden at the White House so beautifully cultivated. And when plans were made for the Carter Center in Atlanta, a rose garden was naturally included. President Carter was such a devoted and loving husband that he would place a fresh rose on her desk each morning. The governor of Hawaii frequently sent tropical flowers, anthurium, ginger, and spray orchids, which Mrs. Carter also liked upstairs. And when she was dressing for a formal affair, Mrs. Carter often requested that a member of her staff call upstairs and report to her the color of the floral centerpiece so that she could coordinate her gown with it.

Today's presidential families use the end of the long upstairs transverse hall as a sitting room. In the 1870s, the hall was divided into three distinct parts: the Guest Quarters, the Central Living Hall, and the West Sitting Room. Originally the Grand Stair rose here in two branches, occupying the entire end of the hall. President Ulysses S. Grant had the stairs changed in 1873 to add floor space on the second floor, and the sitting room developed there over time. When the offices were removed from the east end of the hall to the new West Wing in 1902, the halls became living rooms, flanked largely by bedrooms on the north and south.

President Harry Truman ignored protest and outrage in 1947 when he built a balcony halfway up the tall columns on the southern side of the White House. The "Truman Balcony" has never been considered an architectural improvement; however, first families love using it as their terrace and patio. In the summer, planter boxes are filled with red geraniums along the semicircular edge, sharply contrasting with the white of the house. Comfortable terrace furniture with cushions completes the picture of an inviting family retreat, with perhaps one of the most memorable views in the world.

ABOVE: *This sitting room adjacent to the master bedroom is the one where President and Mrs. Reagan spent most of their time when alone. The room decor is very comfortable, yet it fits in perfectly with the architecture of the White House. In the more formal areas of the second floor, the flower arrangements were more extravagant; however, here on the coffee table is a simple basket of white marguerites. The side tables usually held small flowering plants such as geraniums, violets, or azaleas. Soft ferns usually flanked the mirror above the fireplace.*

BELOW: *In the West Sitting Hall on an April afternoon, First Lady Nancy Reagan reads her mail regarding funding for one of her many charitable causes. A small cachepot filled with simple white marguerites is in the background.*

Regarding the use of floral decorations in the Executive Mansion, Nancy Reagan told *House and Garden* in 1981, "You can have interesting centerpieces without flowers, but, to me, a room without them is sad, almost depressing." She also sincerely appreciated the exciting aspect of working with flowers: "I do enjoy arranging flowers, though I don't have as much time for it as I used to. But now and then, I will arrange a bouquet because I simply cannot resist." One of her favorite flower arrangements was a unique display I created for her dressing table of various-sized bud vases, each with just one or two stems of tuberoses or lilies of the valley. I always enjoyed experimenting with interesting and unusual designs, especially in the family's Residence.

During the Reagan administration, the master bedroom was decorated in soft shades of peach and reds, with a beautiful hand-painted Chinese wallpaper that featured birds and graceful branches of plum blossoms. A pair of Chinese vases with covers pierced with holes to receive flowers decorated the fireplace mantelpiece. Because the wallpaper was fairly busy, I felt that colored flowers would be distracting, so each week I had soft green tree ferns placed in them. One week, the tree fern was not available, so, trying to keep to the oriental theme, I placed curly willow branches in the vases. As luck would have it, it was Sunday and my turn to check all the Mansion arrangements. About 4:30 P.M., as I was making one last look around before leaving for the day, I walked through the second-floor cross hall, and as I passed the President's office, he called out, "Oh, Dottie, come in a minute." I went in, and he said to me, "About those sticks on the mantel." I answered, "Yes, sir?" "Is anything going to happen to them?" Trying to think quickly, I replied, "Yes, sir. I'm going to get rid of them as soon as possible." I guess I had to chalk that one up to my "artistic license" being questioned by a "higher authority." ✍

The South Portico of the White House is not in fact a portico but, lacking a triangular pediment (which would have been difficult with its bow shape) merely a porch. It was added to the house in 1824 by President James Monroe, who set a gardener named Charles Bizet to work planting flowers nearby. This was usually considered the "family" or private face of the White House. Down its stone stairs a frail Andrew Jackson was carried to safety on his inauguration day, fleeing the vast crowds of celebrants that filled the house. The Theodore Roosevelts loved to sit here on summer nights, among the yellow roses that then climbed over the railings. On the South Portico President Franklin D. Roosevelt took his fourth oath of office, about three months before his death. President Harry Truman took the pleasures of the porch upstairs in 1948, when he added the Truman Balcony and cut doors to it from the oval living room on the second floor. That same year the remodeling of the White House began, a work so drastic that when it was done, the Truman Balcony could honestly be called the oldest surviving floor space in the White House.

Michael Deaver confers with President Ronald Reagan in his presidential office on the second floor of the Residence. A small beaker of roses sits on a console table.

Step-by-Step

INTRODUCTION

Since the furniture and personal objects

upstairs in the Family Quarters are changed with each new administration, the ambience can range from a formal setting dictating elegant arrangements in beautiful silver tureens, champagne coolers, or classic Chinese export bowls to a casual atmosphere where almost any type of container may be filled with fresh-cut flowers. Of course, like the First Family's, your upstairs decor may include a bit of both.

Clusters of bud vases on dressing tables, colorful glass beakers in the children's rooms, baskets or bowls of dried flowers, and pots of African violets or other seasonal flowering plants on end tables are favorite choices of many First Family members that can easily become a trademark accent in your private quarters. Today, with the advances in preserving all types of plant materials, it's possible to create an arrangement of freeze-dried roses, gardenias, and lavender with appropriate foliage that will last for months and feel as soft to the touch as their fresh-cut relatives.

In my own home, I frequently fill a container with a selection of freeze-dried roses in colors to complement a room's colors. Although they are rather costly, the fact that they are long-lasting makes them very desirable. In the center of my container I leave a space about 2 to 2½ inches in diameter where I place a favorite statuette. Other times, I fill a juice glass or the cap of a hair spray can with water-saturated foam, place it in the empty space, and fill it in with another complementary shade of roses or maybe two to three sprays of tiny orchids and a bit of bear grass or ivy. This way, I always have something wonderful to use on my tables but still have the option of making it look slightly different every time I wish. ✍

Amber Glass Fan Vase

Fan vases have long been a favorite of flower arrangers, particularly in period rooms. They can sometimes be difficult to arrange because of their extremely slanted sides, which force the flowers to lean to one side or the other. An effective method of securing the stems is to form a grid across the mouth of the container by using clear floral tape stretched in a crisscross fashion, three or four times as needed. Since this container is quite small, I placed one small hydrangea blossom into the center of the opening, then pushed the stems of the other flowers through it as a holder.

5 hot pink nerines
3 stems of white freesia
1 small hydrangea
5 stems of white veronica
1 stem of lady's mantle

1. Place two of the nerines in the vase first: the tallest in the center, a shorter one slightly to the front, with their stems going through the hydrangea.

2. Add the freesias to the left, right, and front.

3. Fill in with the rest of the nerines and veronica, angling some out to the side.

4. Cut the lady's mantle and fill in the arrangement with short pieces.

EAGLE CACHEPOT

7 blue curiosa roses
4 calla lilies
6 white freesia
4 sprigs of pine
12 blue veronicas
Floral foam

1. Fill a cachepot with water-saturated floral foam.

2. Place one rose about 15 to 16 inches tall in the center of the foam, the second about 2 to 3 inches shorter than the first and slightly to the front of the first.

3. Place the remaining roses to the left and right of the center, slightly shorter than the first two, fanning out to the sides.

4. Add the calla lilies out to each side.

5. Then add the freesia and the pine, filling in all of the voids in the arrangement. Finish by inserting the veronicas, with some stalks taller and others slightly shorter. I designed this arrangement to be displayed against a wall, so I made it one-sided.

CORNFLOWER GARLAND

(Adaptation of French Porcelain Seau Créné lé Owned by Thomas Jefferson in 1787)

This is a simple, small arrangement, used in this instance on a bedroom dresser but equally appropriate for the center of a small dining table or even a small mantel.

As in any massed arrangement such as this one, establishing the outline of your finished arrangement is very important. Establish the two sides and the height with some of the smaller flowers and then fill in with the rest.

3 hydrangea heads
8 blue/lavender "Blue Curiosa" roses
4 brodeas
7 stars of Bethlehem
12 white ranunculus
5 calicarpa stems
1 agapanthus
Floral foam

1. Place the hydrangea heads directly down into the center of the foam, reaching about 3 to 4 inches high. This not only helps to hide the foam but gives a good color base into which to work the rest of the flowers.

2. After the hydrangea is placed in the container, cut the agapanthus a bit longer and place it in the center of the container.

3. Continue adding stems to visually support your chosen height and width. Add the roses, brodeas, stars of Bethlehem, and ranunculus in turn, keeping the stems at uneven heights to create depth.

4. The finishing touches are the soft lavender calicarpa stems, placed intermittently among the rest.

SEE-THROUGH LIGHTHOUSE

2 hydrangeas

Water plants, such as water hyacinths

3 agapanthus

4 red twig dogwood branches

4 stems of purple brodea

2 white bouvardia

2 medium-size floral foam-filled cages

Sheet moss

1. Start by soaking the floral foam-filled cages in water and preservative. Then place one of them to the left of a lighthouse sculpture and the other to the right.

2. Pin the sheet moss all around the cages to cover the edges.

3. Place one hydrangea into each cage; it should cover almost the entire cage.

4. Anchor two or three small pieces of water plants into the floral foam-filled cages near the edges.

5. Place one agapanthus into the middle of the hydrangea blossom in the left-hand cage, keeping it fairly tall.

6. Add a couple of dogwood branches and a stem of brodea.

7. Fill in base with bouvardia, short twigs of dogwood, and brodea.

8. On the right-hand side of the arrangement, keep the agapanthus low on the foam base, and add the brodea and twigs to balance.

BLACK SPIRAL VASE

The protea foliage fills in any gaps very nicely. I am a firm believer in using a flower's own foliage whenever possible. The only other addition here is the accent of dogwood twigs, which give it a still more contemporary appeal.

4 large bright red protea
2 to 3 dogwood twigs
Floral foam
Sheet moss

1. Fit the vase with foam and cover it with fresh sheet moss.

2. Place one protea in the center of the foam, keeping it about twice the height of the vase; cut the next protea so that the head will be about 1 1/2 to 2 inches below the first bloom and slightly to either the left or the right.

3. The last one should be placed close to the edge of the vase, preferably lower than and to the opposite side of the last one. Add the dogwood twigs slightly behind the protea, keeping them straight and tall. If the arrangement is to be placed in front of a mirror, insert a fourth protea a bit to the rear so that the arrangement will appear finished in the back.

Prior to a tea with the First Lady of France, Betty Ford escorts Madame Giscard d'Estaing through the second-floor Yellow Oval Room as Nancy Ruwe, Mrs. Ford's social secretary, looks on. They are passing a beautiful arrangement of gerbera, lilies, and marguerites in the Tyler bisque angel compote.

TYLER BISQUE ANGEL COMPOTE

(BETTY FORD WITH NANCY RUWE AND MADAME GISCARD D'ESTAING)

As with all the other historically valuable containers I used in the White House, this compote was fitted with a liner and filled with wet floral foam. You may use recycled plastic tubs from various food items for this purpose in your heirloom containers. The compote itself was not filled in the flower shop, but as with many other original containers, it stayed in its designated location and we merely arranged the flowers in the liner at the flower shop and brought them to the compote.

Peach and yellow gerbera daisies
Orange lilies
Yellow and white marguerites
Floral foam

1. Place the floral foam in a liner.

2. Begin by establishing the height of the arrangement with the tightest orange lily buds.

3. Since the compote is oval-shaped, next add slightly more open lilies on either side to create the dimension of length on either side of the midpoint.

4. Fill in with the remaining gerberas and marguerites, keeping the heavier flowers in prominent positions.

5. Place the liner with the completed arrangement in the container.

6

WHITE HOUSE WEDDINGS

Could there be a more splendid venue for a lavish wedding than the White House? It has every element to make a lucky bride's storybook wedding come true. Since the Kennedy administration, there have been three weddings at 1600 Pennsylvania Avenue, all of them of Presidents' daughters. President Johnson's younger daughter, Luci Baines, married Patrick John Nugent on the very hot, sunny day of August 6, 1966. The marriage ceremony was held at the National Shrine of the Immaculate Conception, the largest Catholic church in the nation. The reception took place afterward in the White House.

Before the noon wedding, Rusty Young and his White House flower staff worked all night decorating the church and the Mansion. Elegant masses of greenery and white flowers were placed throughout the breathtakingly beautiful cathedral. Every fourth pew had bouquets of roses, baby's breath, ivy, alba lilies, and white delphinium attached to the pew ends. These were coordinated with miniature bouquets of the same flowers and greens on the kneelers for the bridal party at the altar. The flower girl carried a basket of roses, and Luci held a bouquet of lilies of the valley, while Mr. Nugent wore a sprig of the same.

Willowy greenery of locust and ficus trees was also used by the White House flower staff to complete the look of a formal garden. These trees were trimmed with white roses, lilies of the valley, and baby's breath. The florists trimmed the trees at the altar into a fancy topiary shape. Two tall silver vases on either side of the altar were filled with white delphinium, alba lilies, and other mixed white flowers. Ropes of green smilax cordoned off the pews that were not used as the building could accommodate 3,500 persons and there were a mere 700 guests! The fragrance of fresh flowers enveloped the church and heightened the romantic atmosphere of this most glorious occasion for the President and his family.

The wedding reception at the White House had a more colorful palette of flowers. Over the Jacqueline Kennedy Garden was extended a white canopy under which the wedding guests assembled before going up to the Blue Room to meet the bridal couple and their parents. The

ABOVE: *Guests at Luci Baines Johnson's wedding enjoy an al fresco reception complete with mixed garden flowers in a small vermeil beaker in the center of the cabaret table.*

LEFT: *Anxious bridal attendants at Luci Baines Johnson's wedding carried small round nosegays of blended pink roses, lilies of the valley, and illusion, while the mother of the bride looks on.*

ABOVE LEFT: *Exquisite pedestal containers filled with large white chrysanthemums, snapdragons, and daisy pompoms set the atmosphere for a lovely wedding buffet in the State Dining Room.*

ABOVE RIGHT: *On the morning of the wedding of her older daughter, Lynda Bird, Lady Bird Johnson gazes up at the chandelier in the State Dining Room, decorated festively with greens, white roses, pompoms, and carnations.*

tent was lined in pink while the poles and ropes were covered with greens and pink and white carnations. A very pretty and whimsical touch was a row of green buckets containing white petunias and pink geraniums along the corridor through which the guests walked to the Blue Room.

The gold chandelier on the ceiling of the State Dining Room formed a marvelous fountain of cascading greens and summer flowers, while the buffet tables were decorated with bowl arrangements of yellow, white, blue, and orange blooms. The buffet table in the East Room had similar arrangements accented by red flowers. Much of the rest of the White House was also exquisitely decorated by the flower staff. Red roses and rubrum lilies, mixed with pink and white flowers, decorated the Red Room, and green nicotiana and lavender stalks along with the requisite pink and white flowers graced the Green Room. And of course, the four magnificent columns and gold torchère in the entrance hall on the State Floor were draped with swags of greenery dotted with flowers. The White House appeared to be a splendid summer garden blooming just for Luci and Patrick.

Helen Taft used the Monroe centerpiece often, describing it as "exceedingly handsome and certainly appropriate to the ceremony with which a State Dinner at the White House is usually conducted." This "surtout" was filled with jonquils and pansies at a dinner held in January 1913 to honor the engagement of the widowed Frances Cleveland to Professor Thomas J. Preston, Jr. of Princeton.

When Grover Cleveland, approaching fifty, married his twenty-one-year-old ward, Frances Folsom, on July 2, 1886, the White House florists spared nothing in making the Mansion a bower of flowers. The Blue Room, where the wedding took place, became a container in itself, massed with flowers and ferns from table to fireplace to gas chandelier. On the hearth the florists put red salvia to denote passion, while in the State Dining Room a temple of Hymen was created on the table to symbolize chastity. Cleveland loved blooming things, and while he sometimes seemed gruff, White House staff now and then would glimpse him bending over to sniff a conservatory tulip or rose.

A little over a year later, the flower staff had to gear up again for another wedding; President Johnson's second daughter, Lynda Bird, married Captain Charles Robb on December 9, 1967. Since the date was close to Christmas, Lynda's flowers were coordinated with the traditional winter holiday decorations at the White House. Bushels of white-tipped holly and regular green holly were brought into the flower shop, along with frosted mistletoe, red carnations, and roses. A Bacarra rose of the same deep, lush red as the Goya crimson shade of the bridesmaid's dresses was used throughout the garlands of greens. Lynda's bridal bouquet was a small, round arrangement of gardenias, white roses, and miniature carnations.

Unlike Luci, Lynda chose to have her ceremony in the East Room, where the color scheme is gold and white. White roses, orchids, gardenias, and frosted mistletoe were placed profusely on the mantelpieces. There were also several topiary trees with clear Italian lights, one pair framing the altar and one in each tall window. The brass stanchions outlining the bridal party's route from the main hall stairway to the altar were decorated with red ribbon bows and small floral arrangements of greens and red flowers. Some other stanchions at different entrances sported twined white and ivory satin ribbons with arrangements of white flowers and white-tipped holly.

ABOVE: *Lynda Bird Johnson in her formal bridal portrait holding a classic clutch bouquet of gardenias, roses, and stephanotis.*

RIGHT: *Lynda Bird Johnson's wedding nuptials in front of an altar created by covering a standing panel with fresh greens backing a white cross.*

The new Mr. and Mrs. Charles Robb on a balcony in the White House during this magnificent Christmastime event.

An important focal point, the main stairway railing, boasted a heavy garland of Christmas greens with a large red-and-white satin ball tucked in among the boughs. All of the first-floor torchères and sconces, as well as the State Dining Room chandelier were decked with red and white carnations. Even the fireplaces were adorned with shiny magnolia leaves. The oval table for the wedding cake was draped in tailored ivory satin and trimmed with a wide white satin ribbon onto which was tacked a garland of white velvet leaves, white satin balls, and frosted mistletoe. In contrast, the buffet tables were trimmed with a wide border of green garland on moss green ribbon. Red and white satin balls were tucked in at intervals along the garland. And on top of the massive five-tiered cake was a basket of white sweetheart roses.

Lynda and Charles also had a beautifully appointed tent in which to entertain their guests. It had a pink lining, a green carpet, and two large windows outlined in black wrought iron with an interesting accent: Mexican paper flowers. The delicate blooms were made in shades of red, pink, and coral and were bunched and tucked into the corners of the framework and around the entranceway. The small tables were covered in pale pink cotton cloths with darker pink skirts and completely surrounded by garlands of natural straw-colored raffia. At intervals all along the raffia, there were clusters of blue and red berries, tiny Christmas figurines, red velvet birds, and shocking pink balls. It made for a magical atmosphere during this glorious time of year.

Nellie Grant, daughter of President Ulysses S. Grant, was married in the White House with the greatest pomp and ceremony. Swagged garlands crossed the East Room, and the state parlors were filled with fine wedding presents, all assembled according to the stores where they had been bought. Lovely Nellie, only a teenager, swept into the room in yards of cream-colored satin, and the groom, a handsome Englishman, awaited her at the altar. Alas, their marriage ended in divorce. Not long after, the next President, Rutherford B. Hayes, and Mrs. Hayes held a full-scale wedding here to renew their vows of twenty-five years before. The press reported that the bride wore the same dress as on her first wedding day, with no mention of alterations. A great floral bell swayed overhead, appeared to be chiming the wedding march after the repronouncement of the devoted husband and wife was made. The next wedding there was Alice Roosevelt's, then two of Woodrow Wilson's daughters, Nell Wilson's bridesmaids carrying tall shepherd's crooks the florist had brightened with orchids. Nell's march began in the East Room, but her vows were spoken in the Blue Room before intimate family members and a mantel banked with orchids and roses.

President Nixon's younger daughter, Tricia, made history when she planned her wedding for the Rose Garden in June 1971. It was the first outdoor wedding ever held at the White House. Though the weather was threatening all day, the rain held off and it turned out to be the social highlight of the Nixon administration and the family's fondest memory from the Executive Mansion. The altar for Tricia's wedding to Edward Cox was an ironwork gazebo fashioned in the White House metal shop. It was covered with hundreds of white roses, her father's favorite, and stephanotis intertwined with a lush green garland.

The chairs for the guests were placed in rows to create a center aisle leading to the altar. The ends of each row were decorated with ribbons and clusters of flowers, while the sides of the aisle were dramatically accented with white French-style tubs made by White House carpenters, filled with gorgeous topiary trees of pink and white roses. Tricia carried a nosegay of white roses and lilies of the valley, and the groom had a lily-of-the-valley boutonniere. Her attendants' bouquets were rather more colorful, with stephanotis, yellow roses, lavender, lilac, and pink geraniums with geranium foliage.

Rusty Young succeeded in making the White House resemble an old-fashioned Valentine with the abundance of romantic flowers throughout the Mansion. Garlands of smilax and gypsophila draped the main stairway. In the East Lobby, there were two very large displays of white mums, alba lilies, roses, carnations, delphiniums, gypsophila,

ABOVE: *In addition to the hundreds of white roses affixed to the ironwork gazebo under which Tricia Nixon and Edward Cox exchanged vows, roses in shades of yellow and pink, as well as nine varieties of white roses, were already blooming in the Rose Garden.*

LEFT: *Well-wishers gaze at the attractive couple Mr. and Mrs. Edward Cox. Several dozen florist volunteers helped to arrange the hundreds of blooms necessary to complete the wedding scene. Nature helped in the Rose Garden by sprouting many pretty flowers, including regal and Madonna lilies, white peonies, geraniums, petunias, and bridal wreath spirea.*

President and Mrs. Nixon express their joy and happiness after the wedding ceremony of their younger daughter, Tricia.

Members of the White House staff photographed the East Room the day President Theodore Roosevelt's daughter Alice married Nicholas Longworth on February 17, 1906. A platform had been built before the great east windows, and mass arrangements on stands were mixed with tubbed palms for decoration, although with some limitation because even the East Room, which measures 40 by 85 feet, was severely pressed to hold so many guests. Ribbons demarcated the standing sections and the aisles through the crowd. Alice carried a massive bouquet, entirely white, and wore a dress with leg-of-mutton sleeves, with a long veil falling from a headdress garland of roses. The bride descended in the elevator and joined her father in the wedding march down the long laurel-banked hall to the East Room.

Cornus Kousa, Japanese tree lilacs, and mock oranges. Two more large arrangements of pink peonies, pink and white carnations, rubrum lilies, lavender and white cushion pompom chrysanthemums, and gypsophila were stationed in the main cross hall. The same flowers were used in the tops of the torchères in the lobby and hall and the chandelier in the State Dining Room. Adiantum fern, gypsophila, stephanotis, and bouvardia were placed around the cake and even made into collars for the Nixons' dogs!

Following the ceremony, Tricia and Edward Cox received their guests in the Blue Room, where two antique vases flanked the doorway. Each was filled with pink and white snapdragons, carnations, roses, rubrum lilies, pink peonies, and lavender pompom chrysanthemums. For the reception in the State Dining Room, the buffet table and mantel were decorated with an assortment of flowers, featuring the white phaelonopsis orchid, named and arranged by Rusty Young's former teacher, Bill Kistler, then director of the American Floral Art School in Chicago. Dancing followed in the East Room, where twenty vermeil beakers containing pink, white, and lavender sweet peas, pink and white snapdragons, pink sweetheart roses, white roses, and adiantum ferns were placed on the cabaret tables.

Both Lynda and Luci Johnson were in attendance to witness Tricia's marriage vows, along with a very special once–White House bride, ninety-eight-year-old Alice Roosevelt Longworth, President Theodore Roosevelt's daughter. She had been married at the Mansion in 1906. The Nixon wedding brought to a close the grand tradition of twentieth-century White House weddings. ✒

Step-by-Step

INTRODUCTION

Flower decorations for a wedding

or bridal shower tend to be lavish and therefore rather laborious in their creation. The traditional color scheme of white and off-whites is always appropriate and adaptable, since it will not clash with any color of bridesmaids' dresses. Today's more informal weddings seem to dictate something different. Still, popular colors such as pink, apricot, and shades of yellow have given way to vibrant, seasonal shades that nicely complement theme weddings. Favorite fall mixes include violet and lavender hues, while shades of blues and greens look splendid in winter.

If you are "doing" a wedding yourself, remember to use the best-quality flowers available within your budget. More is not always better. Clusters of small vases on tables and perhaps potted Boston ferns (for their size) on an altar with just one perfect vase of flowers make a stunning impression. Special attention should be given to prompting any closed buds to open completely by immersing them in hot water before arranging and refrigerating. Although many of the time-consuming, large pedestal or massive buffet table displays are probably best left to professional florists, there are lovely stand-alone arrangements you can make for any wedding.

Garden weddings offer an opportunity for family and friends to get together, gather flowers from the garden, and create tender little clutches for the bride and her attendants. Hand-tied bouquets with ribbon embellishments make lovely decorations for chair backs or the ends of pews, while Victorian-style tussie-mussies in small silver bouquet holders are simply charming. Another novel idea is to use king-sized floral patterned sheets, found in discount stores, tucked and pinned around the dining tables. On top of these, center natural or dyed baskets filled with the same flowers and grasses with which the chair backs are decorated.

When the ceremony or reception is outdoors, it will be necessary to wire the small, delicate flowers and foliage with picks to make tight yet light arrangements that will remain intact even on a windy day. Garlands make a romantic accent around windows, columns, and doorways, and at the edges of ceilings. You may want to wrap real flowers around ropes of silk *faux* ivy because it is easier to work with and less costly and will hold up better. And of course, corsages and boutonnieres make perfectly lovely personal floral touches to give to members of the bridal entourage. ✒

WIRE DRESSMAKER'S BUST

24 calyx leaves
10 pink ranunculus
1 stem of pink rice flower
3 stems of variegated ivy
1 pink feather (optional)
Floral foam

1. Anchor the floral foam to the top of a small dress form by wedging it into the top of the form and securing it with hot glue.

2. Place a ring of small calyx leaves around the lower edge of the form, coming straight out like the brim of a hat.

3. Cut the stems of the ranunculus very short and arrange them to cover all of the foam as well as possible.

4. Fill in any holes with short pieces of rice flower and add a few strands of ivy to hang off to one side, plus a small pink feather if you wish.

Neoclassic Blue Vase

6 mauve miniature calla lilies

7 white nerines

8 stems of white bouvardia

6 freesia

5 pale pink sweetheart roses

2 or 3 stems of lady's mantle

Floral foam

1. Fill the vase with floral foam and place the calla lilies into the foam by spreading the tallest blooms in the center and tapering the others into somewhat of an oval shape.

2. Add the nerines, bouvardia, freesia, and sweetheart roses, keeping them evenly arranged.

3. Finish the arrangement by filling in the gaps with short pieces of lady's mantle.

WEDDING ARRANGEMENT IN COPPER AND SILVER PEDESTAL

6 white "Time Out" lilies

9 white dendrobium orchids

12 white roses

7 white tulips

Several stems of eucalyptus

Floral foam

Moss

1. Fill the container with foam saturated with water and preservative.

2. Stuff moss around the edges of the container to hide the foam.

3. Cut one lily about 15 inches tall and place it in the center back of the container. Cut two more about 12 or 13 inches tall and place them to left and right of the first.

4. Cut the next two lilies about the same length and place them straight out to the left and right foreground along the edge of the container. Cut the last one quite short and face it slightly forward over the front edge of the bowl.

5. Place the dendrobium orchids between the lilies, leaving the stems rather long so that they curve gracefully.

6. Next, evenly distribute the roses and the tulips among the lilies and the orchids. Accent the white flowers with slim pieces of eucalyptus.

WEDDING GARLAND

This garland of fresh flowers has many uses: curved in serpentine fashion down the center of a table, hung as a swag under or on top of a mantelpiece, or twisted through a stair railing.

1 silk ivy garland
25 stephanotis
25 white freesia
Bunch of white wax flowers
6 stems of "Million Stars" baby's breath
Waxed florist's twine

1. Attach the florist's twine to the ivy garland with a knot at one end.

2. Cut the freesia stems to about 4 inches long and break up the wax flowers and the baby's breath into similar lengths.

3. Holding the garland in one hand, gather small clusters of the wax flowers against the garland and wind the twine around the flower stems and the garland, anchoring well.

4. Work your way down the garland, alternating the various types of flowers, including the baby's breath. Be careful to keep the heads of each cluster positioned so that they cover the stems of the previous cluster.

SILVER EPERGNE

A silver epergne of this type is wonderful for a special occasion, such as a wedding buffet table. Instead of flowers, the top may be filled with fruit and nuts, while each hanging basket can hold a votive candle in a glass holder.

12 white roses
12 pink roses
3 stems of white "Time Out" lilies
3 white wax flowers
7 pale pink nerines
4 stems of "Million Stars"
  baby's breath
2 stems of pink floribunda roses
15 stephanotis
10 white tulips
Floral foam

1. Begin by placing foam in the topmost vase and in all of the hanging baskets.

2. In the larger vase at the top, arrange the white and pink roses, the tulips, and the lilies with a couple of the larger wide-open blooms cut off the main stem and placed deep into the arrangement to create a focal point. Try to keep these flowers, as well as the tulips, spread out quite a bit.

3. Then fill in all of the empty spaces with wax flowers and a few nerines. The baby's breath with the stems broken off short acts as a foamy filler.

4. Fill the small baskets with the floribunda roses, the stephanotis, and the rest of the nerines.

5. Finish the look by mounding the shortened baby's breath into the little silver baskets.

A resplendently romantic Victorian portrait is created by a perfect combination of costuming, nostalgic floral displays, and the regal interior design of the Blue Room. The balcony off the Blue Room was decorated with flower boxes containing white geraniums, white petunias, and ivy cascading over the railing.

Historic how-to
BRIDAL BOUQUET

(TRICIA NIXON)

The pedestal arrangements in the Blue Room were arranged very formally in a classic vermeil urn, exhibiting all the right elements. White lilies were placed in the tallest position, while spiky snapdragons radiated outward as a frame. More snapdragons were placed in the center of the arrangement, with pink and white roses and carnations completing the lavish design. Tricia Nixon carried a dainty bouquet of roses and lilies of the valley. Here are the steps to make a similar one.

50 lilies of the valley	*Tissue*
5 white roses	*Ribbon*
Tape	*Bow (optional)*
Wire	

1. With a very fine wire, wrap the short stem of each rose. Then tape the stems together with white floral tape.

2. Since the lily-of-the-valley stems are so fragile, gather them in small clusters of two or three stems, wrap them with a piece of dampened tissue, and then tape them with white floral tape.

3. Gather both the roses and lilies of the valley together in a simple round cluster and wire and tape them.

4. Finally, wrap the "handle" with ribbon and add a bow, if desired, as a finishing touch.

A FIRST FAMILY CHRISTMAS

Christmas is my favorite time of year at the White House. The Executive Mansion never looks more stunning than it does when decorated with bright bows, richly sculpted garlands, and candles or lights sparkling both inside and outside. The smell of fresh evergreens fills the air of every corridor and room. Our work begins very early before the season. We actually determine the decorating theme for the following year immediately after the holiday celebrations end in January. Then, in mid-November, Park Service employees, along with many volunteers and our flower shop staff, begin the tasks of making dozens of mixed-green wreaths and yards of roping to be used throughout the White House. However, the Christmas tree is still the central part of the displays.

Decorated trees had long been a part of German Christmas celebrations when Prince Albert, consort of Queen Victoria, introduced them to the English court in the 1840s. The tradition soon extended across the Atlantic, and the first White House tree was erected in 1889 by President Benjamin Harrison's gardener. It was trimmed simply with candles. Nearly eighty years later, in 1968, for President Lyndon Johnson's last Christmas in the White House, a 20-foot white pine was festooned with gingerbread cookies baked in the White House kitchen by the pastry chef.

Every year, a prizewinning spruce, fir, or pine from the American Christmas Tree Association arrives on the first Wednesday or Thursday of December with much fanfare. It is presented to the First Lady as a gift. On Friday, at the conclusion of the public tours, the Blue Room chandelier is removed and crated for temporary storage. The tree is then hoisted into place, wired directly into the chandelier rosette, and secured at the base.

After carpenters build scaffolding around the huge tree, the electricians begin wiring in the thousands of tiny white lights that will illuminate it both day and night. Then our flower shop staff takes over the painstaking job of attaching the hundreds of ornaments.

Christmas trees look most dramatic when they are decorated according to a theme. Jacqueline Kennedy began that tradition at the White House in 1961, when she chose the *Nutcracker Suite* story as the theme. That year the tree was set up in the Blue Room (not in the East Room, which had traditionally been its home) and trimmed with toy sugarplum fairies, wooden soldiers, tiny musical instruments, and flowers. It was Caroline Kennedy's favorite tree because she was taking ballet lessons. This theme was revisited in 1996 by President and Mrs. Clinton. Mantelpieces were also decorated with *Nutcracker* characters, and the Green Room was decorated in shades of antique pink and Wedgwood blue. Oversized wreaths with a "Twelve Days of Christmas" theme were displayed in the windows along the East Colonnade.

OPPOSITE, CLOCKWISE FROM TOP LEFT:

The first Kennedy Christmas tree, in 1961.

President Nixon's dogs—King Timahoe, Pasha, and Vicki—enjoy having their picture taken in front of the 1971 family Christmas tree in the Residence.

President and Mrs. Bill Clinton pose in front of the White House tree in 1998.

This charming tree in the Blue Room in 1983 depicts a nostalgic Christmas with old-fashioned ornaments of antique toys selected by Nancy Reagan from the same museum from which Mrs. Carter had borrowed ornaments several years earlier.

Up until the Civil War, surprisingly few presidents had young children in the White House. James Madison's stepson was a teenager and John Tyler had one young son, but the first young family really were the three Lincoln boys. After them, children were less of an exception, and at Christmas the White House could be very lively. Fanny Hayes was a lucky little girl who played with a "baby house," completely furnished, in the upstairs corridor. President Benjamin Harrison, in the hundredth year of the presidency, put up what is believed to have been the first White House Christmas tree for his grandchildren, notably the celebrated "Baby McKee," who in his time was the most famous baby in the world.

President John F. Kennedy's daughter, Caroline, enjoying her first White House Christmas tree in the Blue Room in 1961.

Decorating the White House for Christmas is about as American today, in the third century of the house, as Uncle Sam. Few in the large staff of the White House are exempt from helping out. The work originates with the Chief Usher, top executive officer of the residence, the First Lady's office, and the florist shop. Planning begins in early summer for the decorations that will be installed for the following Christmas. Like all White House schedules, this one must be met precisely. Some tasks are performed off-site and the materials are brought in, but most are accomplished in the restricted spaces allotted at the White House.

In decorating for Christmas, as decorating any other time at the White House, no easy way is guaranteed. As the seat of the government, the White House hosts regular activities despite the hectic holiday season. If a last-minute affair of state takes place instead of the decorating, the volunteers just begin when they can, sometimes at three in the morning. Every White House effort proceeds under these circumstances, and every practitioner is a picture of patience and a master of adaptability.

In a typical holiday season, our flower shop was responsible for creating and placing seventy-five double-faced wreaths in the windows, wrapping 2,000 to 3,000 feet of mixed evergreen garlands, and decorating ten to twenty trees of varying sizes, including the 20-foot tree in the Blue Room. The White House also has many historic mantelpieces, which were perfect for displaying the approximately thirty handmade, intricate two- and three-tiered boxwood topiary Christmas trees we made one year. Of course, we never forgot to bring in hundreds of potted poinsettias, in addition to small, festive winter plant arrangements for the many antique tables where flowers were usually placed.

Pat Nixon personally supervised the decorating efforts at the White House. She told *House and Garden* magazine in 1969 that "the tree has lots of meaning, some of the ornaments [eight-inch velvet and satin balls] are decorated with state flowers and people like to walk around and find their state. It's the only cut tree; all the others are in pots and later are planted in a park." One year, Mrs. Nixon placed a precious dollhouse under the tree in the Blue Room. It was the same dollhouse that White House carpenters had fashioned for Fanny Hayes, the daughter of Rutherford B. Hayes, on

Foliage, greens, and floral material come in by the truckload to the White House flower shop, and the staff wastes no time in making the decorations. The woman on the right is Wendy Elasser, who started as a volunteer when I was head of the department during the Reagan administration and is now a full-time employee.

ABOVE: *In the East Room in 1984, about twenty large Christmas trees are trimmed with tiny white lights, glass icicles, preserved baby's breath, and lots of "snow." I decorated the mantels with cut magnolia and other mixed greens around Williamsburg hurricane lamps covering large red pillar candles. The focal point is a set of handmade caroling figures. As a final touch, I set poinsettias in the fireplace.*

ABOVE: *During the Carter Christmas in 1980, I decorated the mantels with single, double, and triple topiaries made with fresh boxwoods on floral foam. I then trimmed them with velvet bows, ivy, and fir while they were on the mantels.*

BELOW: *One of the best things about Christmastime at the White House is the enormous contribution provided by volunteers from all over the country. Here, Nancy Clarke and I direct our volunteers in assembling wreaths on the floor in the cross hall.*

her first Christmas in the White House. It was on loan from the Hayes family and was a great attraction for the children who came to see the tree.

Even though Mrs. Nixon employed the help of Henry Callahan from Saks Fifth Avenue (many First Ladies collaborated with interior designers); Rex Scouten, the White House Chief Usher; and, of course, Rusty Young, the White House Chief Floral Decorator and the horticulturist Irv Williams, she inspired everyone with her own distinct style of dressing up the Mansion. Mrs. Nixon said, "It was my idea to have lots of pots that can be watered easily. Potted miniature ivy makes wonderful garlands across mantels and helps to hide the pots holding poinsettias. Red and white poinsettias all through [the house] turned out to be a great success."

Poinsettias, forced in greenhouses of the National Park Service, are arranged on a special pyramid stand to decorate the stark white halls of the White House at Christmas. Hundreds of these plants are urged to flower by clock-watching gardeners, who, on cue, present them to the florists to set up in the house. The red color is very pleasing in the tall, formal interior of the White House. The color was so popular that President Richard Nixon had the Red Room's color adjusted to match.

Mrs. Nixon introduced many new Christmas customs. In addition to recommending that sixteen wreaths be placed in the windows facing Pennsylvania Avenue, she was the first to hang red, blue, and gold balls from the chandeliers in the halls, which reflected the light from all of the candles. She is perhaps best remembered for establishing the candlelight tours of the White House. In the evening during the holiday season, visitors can view the impressive interior decorations by the soft glow from candles placed throughout the rooms.

These tours have been so popular that each successive First Lady has continued this tradition. Most tourists find it to be their most beautiful memory of the White House. As a champion of American-made crafts, Betty Ford wanted a tree that would showcase the skills of early Americans, so in 1974 she borrowed dozens of hand-carved wooden ornaments from the Abby Aldrich Rockefeller Folk Art Museum in Colonial Williamsburg. The rest of the ornaments were made by volunteers, with additional contributions from individuals and organizations such as 4H clubs, Girl Scouts, and nursing homes across the country.

ABOVE: *Christmas is the perfect time to decorate a chandelier, and here the gold one in the State Dining Room is traditionally appointed with green roping, holly, and boughs of holiday greens for the Nixons in 1973.*

This unique Christmas tree was decorated for President and Mrs. Jimmy Carter by New York designer Louis Nichol. He created the Victorian dollhouse and dressed the antique dolls in pale pink and ivory brocade. The tree stood in the Blue Room in 1980.

Antique toys were placed under the tree, including dolls seated at a tea table and a wooden train from 1800. Flanking the Blue Room door were antique camel and giraffe carousel figures, also from the Rockefeller museum. Our flower room staff completed the White House decorations with period-style mixed greens and fruit arrangements.

The theme of Victorian toys was suggested by Rosalynn Carter in 1978. She borrowed a collection of intricately fashioned toys more than 100 years old from the Strong Museum in Rochester, New York. We decorated the 20-foot fir in the Blue Room with 2,800 miniature toys. Forty larger toys surrounded the base of the tree. It was a monumental task that could have been done only with the help of garden club members from Mrs. Carter's hometown of Plains, Georgia. They traveled to Washington to volunteer their expertise in decorating the Executive Mansion that year. We hung swags of mixed greens and bunches of pine cones along the edges of the ceilings in the East Room, the cross hall in the North Portico, and the State Dining Room. The Carters' daughter, Amy, was also very helpful in furnishing the Victorian dollhouse under the tree.

The Clevelands never had a tree. Theodore Roosevelt's children hung their stockings in an upstairs bedroom that their mother used as a sitting room. But when Ethel Roosevelt, the youngest girl, made her debut at the White House at Christmas of 1908, the vaulted basement halls and adjacent rooms were turned into festive dining rooms with circular tables for eight, each decorated with a Christmas tree centerpiece complete with tinsel and ornaments. Christmas trees as we know them, however, were not annual fare at the White House until the late 1920s.

Even with careful preseason planning, things can go wrong. During one Carter Christmas, we decided to use a healthy quantity of fresh fruit in the green arrangements to create a Della Robbia look. (Luca Della Robbia was a fifteenth-century Italian sculptor who created terracotta reliefs of angels and flowers.) The fruit pyramids on the tables in the State Dining Room, with their luscious apples, lemons, limes, and kumquats, were stunning. The first few days that they were on display, they were fine. Then Washington had one of its unpredictable mid-December heat waves, and fruit flies took over the large room. We had to redo everything in permanent fruit. Needless to say, from that day on, fruit has generally been used only for special events of short duration.

In 1981, the Reagans' first Christmas in the White House, I decorated the foyer on the ground floor with cyclamen, pink poinsettias, and a profusion of narcissus, as I had done in the previous administration for the Carters. Narcissus was Rosalynn Carter's favorite scented flower. When the Reagans approached this area on their "walk-through" to preview the decorations, the President started to sneeze. We were all unaware of his allergy. The walk-through did continue, and the plants were relegated to areas that he frequented less often.

ABOVE TOP: *First Lady Hillary Clinton and Chief Floral Decorator Nancy Clarke discuss the Christmas embellishments to the Monroe plateau on the State Dining Room table as the press gets its first glimpse of the annual decorations. A matching opulent topiary of artificial fruit stands at one end of the room.*

ABOVE BOTTOM: *Poinsettias are almost always used upstairs in the Family Quarters, and here President and Mrs. Bill Clinton have added some garland and tinsel around the magnificent doorways in the center hall along with poinsettias in cachepots flanking the door.*

BELOW: *The North Entrance Hall during a Reagan Christmas in 1982; in addition to the yards of roping made of mixed greens, the combination of deeply hued poinsettias and rich red carpet makes a boldly festive statement. To add some holiday shimmer, I placed trees covered with hundreds of bee lights in the corridor niches.*

ABOVE: *A visitor to the White House is greeted by a storybook winter scene of trees with bee lights and "snow" in the North Foyer looking toward the Blue Room during the Bush administration in 1991.*

That same year, Nancy Reagan and I chose handmade ornaments from the American Folk Art Museum in New York City. She very much enjoyed trimming the 19-foot tree in the Blue Room with our flower shop staff. In addition, I needed the help of thirty volunteers to decorate the rest of the Mansion with poinsettias, holly, and evergreens, not to mention two trees with real, unlit candles in the North Entrance Hall and six trees with tiny white lights in the East Room. The mantelpieces held mixed greens, lotus pods, and apples. One serving table sported topiary trees made of apples on top of silver ice buckets. I completed the "old-fashioned Christmas" look with a dollhouse created by interior designer Aline Koplin Gray of Philadelphia and an exquisite Italian baroque crèche given as a gift to Lady Bird Johnson in 1967.

Outside, on the Ellipse in front of the White House, ten thousand mostly blue lights sparkled on the national Christmas tree. It was topped with a unique decoration of thirteen large stars, symbolizing our country's original thirteen colonies.

ABOVE: *For a State Dinner in 1982 in honor of the President of Pakistan, the mirror above the East Room mantelpiece made a beautiful backdrop for a vermeil soup tureen arranged with peach and ivory gerbera, ivory euphorbia, and magnolia foliage.*

T he Christmas season is a memorable time at the White House. Two centuries ago, little was remarked about it. Indeed, sometimes Congress even met on Christmas Day. But as the nineteenth century progressed, the holiday celebrations took the form of open houses, family dinners, and religious services. President Calvin Coolidge put up the first national Christmas tree in 1927 in Lafayette Park, across the street from the White House. The actual name was not devised until 1941, when, in the wake of Pearl Harbor and the declaration of war, President Franklin D. Roosevelt insisted that there be a "national tree." Discouraged for security reasons from going to the park, he ordered the Christmas tree set up on the South Lawn. Before thousands of spectators, he pushed the lighting button on the South Portico, and at the sight of the blazing tree, the crowd burst into carols. Winston Churchill, who had been on the porch with the President, then emerged into the light, thus announcing his presence in the United States, which had not been known.

For another Reagan Christmas, we coordinated our decorations with the eightieth anniversary of the teddy bear (appropriate for the White House since it was named for President Theodore Roosevelt). For our tribute to "old Teddy" we trimmed the tree with hundreds of Steiff teddy bears and antique toys. Our most creative design within this theme was the construction of 4-foot pyramidal topiary trees of boxwood fashioned in white French tubs made for us by the White House carpentry shop.

We covered the small trees with more teddy bears dressed in Colonial-type garb handmade by my assistant, Nancy Clarke. Even the wreaths throughout the Mansion had teddy bears hanging from them. The bears appeared to have invaded the White House. As it turned out, our celebration was a bit premature (actually on the "eve" of the anniversary year), but we happily took credit for leading the way in our nation's tribute to the cute little bears.

A most moving Christmas season for me, personally, was with the participation of members from Second Genesis, a group home for recovering drug addicts. The White House's association with this organization evolved from Mrs. Reagan's efforts with her "Just Say No" anti-drug campaign. Our flower shop staff had been planning all year with the Origami Society of New York to feature handmade origami ornaments on the Blue Room tree. Its members had worked just as long on this project. Mrs. Reagan suggested that we use some volunteers from the Second Genesis home to help us complete the task of making some of the less intricately folded ornaments.

So about ten volunteers, guarded by uniformed Secret Service agents, worked side by side with Nancy Clarke and myself in the flower room. Most of these addicts were on their "last chance." They had all committed crimes, many of them serious, and simply couldn't believe that they were allowed to be in the White House. They told us their stories of their addictive lives, and it was very evident that their feeling of self-worth was extremely low or nonexistent.

It was heartwarming to witness that as the weeks passed and they made the delicate ornaments, their attitudes changed. Mrs. Reagan invited them to the volunteer Christmas party so they could see how their efforts had made a beautiful contribution to a White House Christmas. I often think of those young people and hope that perhaps our giving them a chance to do something they could be proud of made a difference in their future lives. 🖋

The "Second Genesis" tree was decorated with origami ornaments made of brightly colored metallic paper, 100 balls embellished with velvet lace and ribbon, yards of shiny beaded roping, and many tiny white lights.

Step-by-Step

INTRODUCTION

wreaths on doors and windows. This tradition began in Scandinavia as a token of peace, renewal, and friendship. My own preference for making wreaths, and one that I always used at the White House, requires a wire box frame into which wet sphagnum moss is placed, then wrapped with green wax paper and secured with green florist twine. A wreath should be hung up overnight to allow any excess water to drip out. Fresh-cut foliage will last much longer when made in this fashion. A foam ring may be substituted for the wire frame. In this case, the stems of greenery are inserted into the dampened foam. One lovely idea for a special occasion over the holidays is to enhance a mixed green arrangement of incense cedar, blueberry juniper, holly, and pine with fresh-cut flowers.

Garlands, too, are a nostalgic element in holiday decorating and can capture different moods depending on the foliage you choose, from contemporary and exotic to traditionally elegant. I love using holly, ivy, or mistletoe because of their winter-producing berries. But if a garland is to last a week or more, using ivy or other soft foliage wrapped around the nylon florist's rope is probably not the best choice. Longer-lasting materials include fir, juniper, pine, and cedar, as well as the aromatic herbs rosemary and eucalyptus. Mixing those greens in varying proportions as you wrap them with wire along the length of the rope will create different looks.

Interspersing twiggy branches that have been sprayed with silver or gold paint, or covered in moss or lichen with greens, gives a wonderfully natural country effect. A garland may also be made with dried baby's breath or dried hydrangea for a nearly permanent decoration. As with wreaths, garlands may be formed by using the same technique of wrapping damp floral foam in chicken wire and securing it in a tubular shape with wire. This method works quite nicely for making garlands that will be placed on a table or mantelpiece.

Topiaries, in various forms, date back to early Greek and Roman times. They can be seen in frescos in Pompeii and on fragments of Greek pottery. They may be made of trained live plants such as ivy, creeping fig, and herbs such as rosemary. Fanciful ones on Styrofoam balls or wet floral foam are especially fun to make.

A traditional Christmas topiary may be created in a clay pot or in a much more elegant container using a commercial topiary form studded with boxwood. I like to use a block of floral foam shaped into a cone, saturated with water and a preservative, then inserted with small pieces of greens such as boxwood plus red berries and a bit of holly. This "tree" can last all through the holidays if you take it to the kitchen sink and spray it occasionally. ✍

BRASS PEDESTAL BOWL

This holiday arrangement is very festive without resorting to the traditional red and green, which many times clash with the colors of a room. The use of the preserved chestnuts, hanging amaranthus, and rosemary (for remembrance) are also rather untraditional touches.

6 pink Madelon lilies
4 double tuberoses
12 pale pink Melani roses
Some sprigs of holly
½ bunch of preserved rosemary
Bunch of mixed Christmas greens
  (cedar and pine)
6 preserved chestnuts
2 preserved green hanging amaranthus
Floral foam
Floral tape
Wooden picks

1. Fill the bowl with floral foam that has been soaked with water and preservative. Keep the foam slightly over the top of the container (1 inch), and anchor it with floral tape.

2. Place the tallest lily in the center and one each at two o'clock and eleven o'clock, with the other two resting on the edge of the container. Complete filling in with the remaining lilies on both the left and right sides.

3. Place the tuberoses on either side of the central lily.

4. Then fill in empty spaces with the roses, holly, rosemary, and mixed greens.

5. Either wire or hot-glue the chestnuts onto 6- to 12-inch wooden picks and place them where they can be seen to the best advantage.

6. Add the hanging amaranthus over the side of the container, where it will provide the perfect accent.

CHRISTMAS GARLAND

For this particular stairway I used 2 yards of plaid taffeta material and split it into three strips. The pale mauve panné velvet was a remnant that I split similarly.

Cut fresh pine, fir, or other evergreens
1 artificial green garland, 6 to 9 feet long or
*   whatever length is needed for your stairway*
5 small mauve/pink flowering kales
3 to 4 long pieces of preserved hanging
*   amaranthus*
Bunch of money plant
4 dozen pink freeze-dried roses
Dried blue hydrangea heads
2 bags of fresh cranberries
Spool wire
Flocked wire
2 yards plaid taffeta
Short remnant of mauve velvet

1. Cut the evergreen boughs into pieces about 6 to 7 inches long.

2. Secure the wire to one end of the garland and start placing clusters of greens against it, attaching them with the wire wrapped tightly around both. Keep on adding the greens in mixed clusters, each cluster of greens laid over the stems of the previous grouping and wired in tightly. Continue until the entire garland is completely covered, ending with a cluster or two of greens attached in the opposite direction so the ends look finished.

3. Using flocked wire, gather the plaid taffeta and the garland and attach it to the bottom newel post, leaving a long end to hang down gracefully.

4. Next, drape the garland and "ribbons" of taffeta up the stairway to the top.

5. Attach a flowering kale, the hanging amaranthus, the pale pink roses on short wire stems, pieces of money plant, and the hydrangea heads. As you work your way up the garland, add in the roses, the hydrangea, and the money plant.

6. Place another flowering kale at each spot where the garland is anchored to the banister.

7. String the cranberries on beading wire to make a flexible garland to weave in and out of the green garland.

8. Add the cranberry garland and a bow made of the mauve velvet and the taffeta to the newel post.

CAPITAL STONEWARE VASE

This container has a great deal of appeal and is very effective for a house with classical styling or even an eclectic decor. You may find a similar piece by searching in a salvage yard that sells architectural pieces. Here it is used at the Christmas season in a very interesting hallway accented by some of the owner's remarkable collection of *santos*.

Plastic container
2 dozen red roses
5 branches of holly
10 strands of ivy
1 bag cranberries
Floral foam
Beading wire

1. This simple arrangement begins with a plastic container anchored to the top of the capital and filled with foam.

2. Place one or two dozen roses in the foam-filled holder, massing them in a triangular shape. Make sure that throughout the arrangement some of the roses are shorter and placed more deeply into the arrangement.

3. Add the holly and the ivy strands for contrast. When using holly with fresh flowers, I like to trim off the sharp points of the holly with shears so that the flowers' delicate petals won't be damaged.

4. String the cranberries on beading wire, loop them in a bow shape, and wire them to a 6-inch pick. Then insert the pick into the foam. Because the cranberries are on wire, they may be bent and manipulated around the flowers to display them to the best advantage.

OLD GLORY WREATH

Twig wreath base
Preserved rosemary, cedar, reed grass, holly, and green amaranthus
5 preserved chestnuts
Spanish moss
Glue gun
Flag-patterned ribbon
Flocked wire

1. Using a purchased twig wreath base, glue in mixed pieces of the preserved greens, tucking them into the twigs and anchoring well.

2. Make a large bow with two to four loops, depending on the width of the ribbon. Secure the bow with flocked wire and attach to the bottom of your wreath.

3. Add the preserved chestnuts and bits of Spanish moss to lighten the dark colors a bit. Twist a loop of wire at the top for hanging.

One year, on the eagle-based pier tables in the State Dining Room,
I had the White House carpenters fashion French tubs into which we
placed 3 1/2-inch boxwood topiaries, covered them with moss, and
added shiny, red apples, accented with teddy bears.

Historic how-to

APPLE TOPIARY

For the eightieth anniversary of the teddy bear, Nancy Reagan decided to have a teddy bear theme for the White House Christmas decorations. These topiary trees were designed for the pier tables in the State Dining Room and were accented with wonderful Steiff bears dressed in handmade Colonial-style clothing. The carpentry shop made handsome French-style tubs, but you may use any sturdy flat-bottomed container that will be proportionately the right size for the height of your topiary.

Boxwood

Red wax apples

Teddy bears or other ornaments

Floral foam

Dowel

Chicken wire

Wooden picks

1. Fill the container with blocks of wet floral foam and then pack more foam up and around a center dowel that has been secured into the bottom. Wrap this entire structure with chicken wire and secure it with wire.

2. Insert cut pieces of boxwood into the damp foam to create the "tree." I like to work from the top down, adding long pieces that stand straight out of the top and then gradually working my way down to form a conical shape. Continue sticking pieces of boxwood into the foam and wrapping downward until you create what looks like a cone-shaped boxwood tree planted in the tub.

3. Wire shiny red wax apples onto wooden picks and insert them throughout the "tree."

4. Attach teddy bears or other ornaments wherever they look best.

CELEBRATIONS

To any guest who has ever entered the columned grandeur of the White House, every experience seems like a celebration. The staff works very hard to ensure that, within the framework of that experience, flowers are used creatively to enhance the event. As a floral designer, I naturally think of flowers in the context of an arrangement or centerpiece. The White House kitchen staff came up with a unique, charming use for fresh flowers in an artistic culinary creation. The Flowerpot Sundaes made their debut at Luci and Lynda Johnson's bridesmaid parties, and, due to popular demand, were adopted by Mrs. Johnson for her entertaining.

Of course the premier ceremony of the presidency is the inauguration, in which the power the successful candidate has won in the election is confirmed by the American people and he takes an oath to use it properly. Inaugurations are held at the Capitol. Before 1960, three were held at the White House. In 1841, John Tyler took the oath, probably in the office upstairs, even as black crape was being tacked up over the chandeliers and mirrors below for the dead President William Henry Harrison. Rutherford B. Hayes, whose inauguration day was overshadowed by the fear of rioting over his disputed election, took his oath in the Red Room in 1876. In January 1945, an ailing President Franklin D. Roosevelt took his fourth oath on the South Portico.

Immediately following the inauguration, the President goes to the White House for the first time as President of the United States. His predecessor has cleared out entirely. The house is decorated with flowers, and a luncheon is served that in early years was planned by the outgoing President and First Lady. Long ago, when inaugurations were held in early March, the house was simply opened to the public after the President arrived. Sometimes many thousands of people came to call. The most famous inaugural reception was that of Andrew Jackson in 1829, when, because Jackson's theme was the "common man," many people called at the house who would not have felt comfortable doing so previously. The crowd swelled to many thousands, and the result was a near riot. The President was hustled to safety in a hotel. To empty the house, the steward placed washtubs filled with bourbon and orange juice on the south grounds, and the rush was on.

As part of her Beautification Program, she regularly hosted luncheons in the Family Dining Room for the staff and volunteers who worked with her on this nationwide effort to preserve scenic wilderness and plant bulbs and trees in inner-city parks. Mrs. Johnson's favorite sundae was a sweet but light concoction of homemade ice cream, sponge cake, and meringue layered in a terra-cotta flowerpot. Then, through the middle, was inserted a clear drinking straw into which was placed a single rose or tulip stem. These miniature sundaes were the perfect dessert as well as floral decoration!

As for the menu, careful planning is usually required for the decorations at a celebration. However, crises do occur, and a seasoned floral designer is always up to the task. In January 1985, for the second inauguration of Ronald Reagan, the weather in Washington turned miserable, and on the day of his swearing-in there was so much snow on the ground that the streets of the capital were virtually impassable. The swearing-in customarily takes place at noon on the steps of the Capitol, but when it became evident that reaching those steps would not be possible, it was decided to have the Presi-

President Ronald Reagan hosts a luncheon in the Rose Garden in honor of the astronauts of the space shuttle Columbia *in 1981. This patriotic arrangement features a white basket brimming with white lilies, blue bachelor's buttons, and miniature red carnations.*

dent sworn in on the grand staircase in the White House and then go to the Capitol as soon as a path could be cleared.

I was briefed on this change of plans and told that there would be an impromptu reception in the State Dining Room following the swearing-in. As the kitchen readied the coffee and cookies and the butlers prepared the table with a long lace cloth, I started to rack my brain for something significant to use on the center of the table. One of my very favorite pieces in the White House collection is a large silver boat with sails. It was created by the Gorham Silver Company and is a replica of Hiawatha's boat from Longfellow's poem. I launched it full of white roses, always on hand in the flower shop, freesia, stars of Bethlehem, and some ivy trailing over the sides. It looked stunning, and I was proud to have contributed so ingeniously to this historic moment.

ABOVE: *Jacqueline Kennedy gives her husband, President John F. Kennedy, a piece of the White House lawn on his birthday in 1963. He had requested that Jackie create a Rose Garden on the South Lawn for outdoor ceremonies.*

BELOW: *Easter is always delicious as well as beautifully decorated at the White House. President and Mrs. Bill Clinton delight in the festive floral decorations and the glorious pastries created by Chef Roland Mesnier.*

One of the most compelling and symbolic ceremonies of the White House is the receiving of credentials of foreign diplomats by the President. Thomas Jefferson devised the ceremony in 1801, when the highest-ranked diplomat to the United States was a minister plenipotentiary. Our second President, who opposed any kind of official ceremony on philosophical grounds, nevertheless yielded slightly in this case and positioned himself in the center of the Blue Room. When the mahogany doors to the hall were thrown open, the diplomat would enter with his aides and the President would receive the commission papers, sumptuous handwritten, gold-sealed parchments that had been signed by the King, Queen, or other head of state whom the diplomat represented. They did not bow to Jefferson as they had to George Washington and John Adams, but shook hands. With this innovation, Jefferson ended forever the debate as to whether shaking hands was or was not suitably respectful of the President as head of state.

The ceremony has changed little in two centuries. On the day of the presentation, the President takes his place in the center of the Blue Room, with his official family placed formally behind him. The Secretary of State brings the diplomat to the room, where the papers are presented. After cordial addresses by each party, the group retires to the State Dining Room for refreshments.

The lavish horizontal arrangement of mixed roses and ivy on a splendidly draped dais becomes a focal point for this special event, a formal luncheon for President Nelson Mandela of South Africa, hosted by President and Mrs. Clinton.

America's Bicentennial celebration brought the busiest season of entertaining to the White House that the nation had ever seen. During the summer of 1976 there were as many as two State Dinners a week! A huge white tent was erected in the Rose Garden under which as many as 250 guests could be seated. Many world leaders came to extend Bicentennial good wishes, including Queen Elizabeth II of Britain, King Juan Carlos and Queen Sofia of Spain, Prime Minister Malcolm Fraser of Australia, and Chancellor Helmut Schmidt of Germany. One such dinner was in honor of President Valéry Giscard d'Estaing of France on the occasion of his visit with his wife to President and Mrs. Ford in May 1976.

It was a white-tie dinner for 160 very special guests. Betty Ford selected an early American lighting collection as the centerpiece theme. This featured lanterns, candelabra, and candlesticks made of tin, brass, pewter, and wrought iron. Arrangements of anemones, Mrs. Giscard d'Estaing's favorite, along with sweet Williams, lilacs, rubrum lilies, sweetheart roses, and heather, accented the lighting pieces. As an expression of our gratitude to France for its two hundred years of alliance, we decided to cover the tables with a reproduction of a French cotton textile from around 1775. The original design of red and blue wildflowers on an ecru background is on display in New York City's Metropolitan Museum of Art.

Perhaps the most challenging event for the White House flower shop staff was the sit-down dinner honoring 1,300 released American prisoners of war given during the Nixon administration. It required far more arrangements than any other celebration I can recall. The South Lawn was awash in bright orange and yellow tents; the largest measured 100 by 180 feet and enclosed 130 tables for ten, each needing a centerpiece. The center stage was also decorated. Two other tents were set up to seat 650 guests in each. In addition, each State and Diplomatic floor sported more than fifty fresh floral arrangements. Everyone on staff at the White House worked more efficiently than ever to make this evening especially memorable for the brave prisoners of the Vietnam War. The color scheme for the tables was dictated by the rich yellow cloths, and Rusty Young designed handsome arrangements of carnations, marigolds, roses, and daisies in shades of red, orange, yellow, and white. Low lighting for each table was provided by two white candles in hurricane lamps.

At a State Dinner in December 1979 honoring Prime Minister Margaret Thatcher of the United Kingdom, the centerpiece featured her favorite flowers: anemones mixed with lilac, euphorbia, and French heather. All of the ladies attending the gala evening received a tussie-mussie as a favor to take home.

During the Kennedy administration, innovator Letitia Baldrige, who was head of the Office for the First Lady, revived a tired state reception ceremony by turning the South Portico into a handsome stage to welcome important foreign guests of the President. Previously the guests had arrived at a nearby military airport, then been driven in a parade to the White House, with government workers let out from work to watch and wave flags. This absorbed valuable hours. The new approach was to bring the guest by helicopter to the South Lawn, where a pageant awaited. Some six hundred spectators had been admitted. Driven to the South Portico, the guest was greeted by the President and First Lady; guest and President then ascended a small platform, each delivering a brief address. The Marine Band then played. And the ceremony was over in about twenty-two minutes!

ABOVE LEFT: *In the Oval Office, President Jimmy Carter talks with President Gerald Ford during the presentation of President Ford's official White House portrait. The colorful coffee table flowers are gerberas, delphiniums, bachelor's buttons, snapdragons, and roses.*

ABOVE RIGHT: *On a typically hot Washington July day, Vice President and Mrs. Dan Quayle and Mrs. George Bush enjoy a picnic luncheon commemorating the twentieth anniversary of the United States' landing on the moon. A log basket filled with pretty, all-white flowers with small American flags complements the traditional red-and-white-checked tablecloths.*

LEFT: *Peach garden roses, smilax, and limes intertwine into a long, delicate arrangement that extends the length of a very historic head table for the White House Historical Association Dinner to celebrate the two hundredth anniversary of the White House in November 2000. Betty Ford is seen here talking with former President Jimmy Carter. Lady Bird Johnson, Rosalynn Carter, President and Mrs. George Bush, and President and Mrs. Bill Clinton were also in attendance.*

Sometimes the setting for a special event is a location off the grounds of the White House. For the Summit of Industrialized Nations in the summer of 1983, President Reagan's staff planned the event to take place in historic Williamsburg, Virginia. It was a most difficult assignment because only my assistant, Nancy Clarke, and I were given clearance to work the weekend event in the unfamiliar surroundings. The kitchen of the College of William and Mary served as our flower shop, and we had to get used to traveling between the White House and Williamsburg in a helicopter. Due to the normally very public venues in Williamsburg, security at the summit was extra tight, and our flower staff station wagon had to endure several checkpoints between our "shop/kitchen" and the tables set up underneath an immense white tent outside. On the way to deliver the arrangements for a very important luncheon at the Governor's Mansion, an overzealous guard dog sniffing for explosives decided to jump right in and began stomping all over the flowers! He was eventually coaxed out, but Nancy and I had only minutes to remove the broken stems and adjust the arrangements. The centerpieces looked lovely, and I'm sure no one noticed that we had averted another tablescape crisis.

A mong the earliest visitors to the White House were the Native Americans so ardently courted by the Presidents and their governments for their integral place in the great West that presumably lay open for settlement. Often the tribes were brought to Washington at government expense. A ceremony at the White House always accompanied these visits of state. Thomas Jefferson, who was very interested in the West, was the first President to greet Indian delegations, and he did so in the great entrance hall, the largest available space. Speeches were exchanged very formally. The chiefs presented gifts, and the President presented silver medals.

The tradition was continued, and the ceremonies were numerous. James Monroe was asked by one delegation to hang the gifts they had brought on the walls of his "lodge" (the White House) so that their grandchildren could go there and see them. Every President through nearly the end of the nineteenth century went through these meetings, until the West was considered "settled" and the matter of Indian relations had been reduced to the severe suppression of objectors.

Jacqueline Kennedy entertains President Mohammad Ayub Khan of Pakistan at a State Dinner given in his honor at Mount Vernon, Virginia, the home and burial place of George Washington, on July 11, 1961. Each table held a simple garden arrangement of carnations, belladonna, gallardia, and daisies.

It's not only First Ladies who become involved in floral decoration for special events. Often their children love the art form, too. When Susan Ford had her Holton Arms senior prom at the White House, we all had fun helping her. Susan and her friends actually made all of the decisions about the invitations, food, music, and so on, but they turned to our flower shop to create the table centerpieces. They set up small cabaret tables in the East Room, decorated them with little hurricane candle holders, and adorned each with a ring of small mixed flowers at the base. About eight of Susan's friends came down to the flower shop and, with a little coaching from us, arranged every single stem handily.

There is a wonderful story told by Bess Abell, Social Secretary to Mrs. Johnson. She recalled that on one occasion Elspeth Rostow, the wife of Walter Rostow, President Johnson's National Security Adviser, made a dismaying discovery as she entered the White House for a formal function. On her way up the stairway from the Diplomatic Reception Room to the main floor, there was the usual bottleneck as guests were given their seating cards on the top landing. While she and Walt were at the foot of the stairs, she looked up and saw another woman wearing the same dress she was. She quickly realized that this guest was not going to be too happy that someone else had on the identical white lace dress with a turquoise sash. So she disappeared into the ladies' room to try to figure out what to do.

There on a dressing table was a bowl of anemones and some safety pins. Elspeth took off the sash, pinched off the stems of several anemones, tacked them at her waist with the pins, and exited the ladies' room with a stunning new look. She then went back through the receiving line and into the State Dining Room and sat down to dinner. About halfway through the meal, she looked down to find that her anemones were beginning to wilt and the pins were beginning to show.

Noticing a lovely bouquet of flowers as the centerpiece, she discreetly took a few out of the arrangement, pinched off their stems while holding them under the table, and switched the fresher, sturdier flowers for the wilted anemones. So by the end of the meal, she had an entirely new waist of pretty blossoms.

After the dinner, as the guests were going into the East Room for entertainment, a woman approached her and said, "I'm going crazy! I'm sure you had red and blue flowers at your waist, and now you have apricot and bronze flowers at your waist. I don't understand that. I thought I had a very good visual memory." I always knew that a beautiful display of fresh flowers never fails to make a lasting impression! 🖉

Here I am in a proud moment when President George Bush visited me in the White House flower shop.

Step-by-Step

INTRODUCTION

of year at the White House, there are many other holidays and occasions that call for special floral designs. St. Patrick's Day was generally celebrated with a visiting representative of the Irish government. A dinner or luncheon was planned, but sometimes it was just a reception. Of course the predominant color was always green. Pots of shamrocks and bowls of green and white carnations with Bells of Ireland were placed throughout the Executive Mansion. A simple yet effective arrangement to make in your home for a family or social meal is a St. Patrick's Day potato place marker. Hollow out a 2- to 2½-inch opening in a large baking potato and insert a small pot of shamrocks in the well. Add a small green bow on a pick with your guest's name on it, and you have a novel table decoration.

Easter is always a spectacular celebration at 1600 Pennsylvania Avenue. Painted eggs autographed by famous sports figures and celebrities are hidden on the White House grounds for children to gather into baskets during the Easter Egg Hunt. A colored-egg centerpiece, perhaps in a low glass dish with moss nestling the beautiful eggs, can be made even more enjoyable by cracking open several eggshells that were emptied before staining, spooning in some dirt, and planting tiny Johnny Jump-ups or little tête-à-tête narcissus in them. Then tuck these diminutive floral "pots" in among the whole colored eggs. ✍

Dining Table
Collection

The same general directions may be followed using entirely different candleholders, bowls, and figures. Think of using rather crudely made Mexican pottery, or, if you are fortunate enough to have a few pieces of alabaster or marble you could create a very elegant look. If using alabaster or marble be sure to use a liner for your foam, since often they are not waterproof.

This tablescape has endless possibilities. Here I have used fine crystal, but almost any clear glass may be used.

1 fine crystal bowl
2 fine crystal eagles
1 tall fine crystal pillar candlestick
2 6- or 8-inch candlesticks for flowers
2 candlesticks for tapers
2 6-inch pillars with 3-inch candles
4 pieces floral foam
Posy clay

3 to 4 white hydrangea
10 to 12 roses
½ bunch white nerines
2 bunches white freesia
2 bunches white bouvardia
½ bunch lady's mantle

1. Begin by placing floral foam on the tops of three candlesticks of different heights, attaching them with posy clay. Hot glue may also be used.

2. Cover the foam with the hydrangea separated into short pieces and pushed tightly into the foam.

3. Then fill in with short stems of roses, three for each candlestick. I chose to use slightly open roses for a more lush look.

4. Lastly add the nerines, freesia, and bouvardia, all cut fairly short. Be careful to arrange them so that each flower may be seen and enjoyed.

5. Finish off by cutting up the lady's mantle and tucking the short pieces in to set off the all-white flowers. The large bowl that is the main component of this arrangement has a wide, flat bottom where I was able to place the magnificent crystal eagle.

6. To one side of the bowl, place another foam cage, anchoring it with posy clay. Put in one large white hydrangea to almost cover the cage, making it easy to hide the mechanics (the foam cage).

7. Insert stems through the hydrangea; add the roses, nerines, and veronica low down and swept to one side, and finish off with spreading tendrils of ivy.

8. Fit the rest of the candlesticks with candles and move all pieces about the table until a pleasant combination of flowers and candle heights is achieved.

GARLANDED ROMAN BUST

Pink rice flowers

Hydrangeas

Light pink nerines

Red and yellow crab apples

Eucalyptus

White bouvardia

2 red roses

2 peach roses

2 peach spray roses

Lily

Variegated ivy

Veronica

Wax flower

Star of Bethlehem

Waxed twine

Hank of long raffia, about 20 to 35 strands,
  or a permanent ivy garland

1. Anchor the twine to the end of the hank of raffia or permanent ivy garland and start attaching flowers by winding the twine around the raffia and the flower stems.

2. Try to keep the heads of the flowers overlapping the stems of the previously attached ones. Make the garland fairly thick and opulent-looking, mixing the flowers well. As you reach the end, leave slightly longer ends of raffia to hang down on one side.

STARS AND STRIPES IN GLASS

This type of arrangement is best made "in place" so that the flowers, though an important feature, do not overpower the beautiful crystal sculpture.

> *3 agapanthus*
> *5 blue veronicas*
> *6 red roses*
> *7 to 9 white bouvardia*
> *5 pieces variegated ivy*
> *7 stars of Bethlehem*
> *1 stem of white wax flower*
> *3 to 4 blue brodeas*
> *2 floral foam holders*

1. Place the 2 floral foam holders on either side of your sculpture. In this case the left side was the more prominent one, so I placed one large agapanthus about twice the height of the sculpture into the foam, then a second, cut very short, to the right at the base partially covering the foam.

2. Next, place one veronica into the foam just above the agapanthus to give the whole arrangement a sharp clear line.

3. Then add four of the red roses and continue filling in with the other flowers, extending the longer types, stars of Bethlehem, and veronica almost horizontally out to the left side.

4. Last, add the short pieces of wax flower and the ivy to any areas where the foam was exposed.

5. Arrange the other floral foam holder in a similar fashion, but smaller and lower.

DANCING FIGURES

If you are using this type of arrangement as a centerpiece for a luncheon or dinner table, be sure to keep turning the foam adapter around as you work.

3 artist's models, about
*   12 inches high*
5 pale pink nerines
11 kyria roses
3 stems of floribunda roses
3 stems of pink rice flower
short pieces of eucalyptus
2 foam adapters
Wire
Fresh sheet moss

1. Make hairpins out of wire and push through the moss into the foam to hold. This will help hide the foam adapters.

2. Place a nerine in the center of the foam adapter, slightly taller than the models.

3. Next add a couple of kyria roses, cut a little shorter.

4. Cut the floribunda buds and flowers off the main stem and place them low into the arrangement. Fill in with more kyria roses, nerines, and rice flower.

5. Finish with the eucalyptus to help set off the lovely pale shades of pink.

6. Make the next foam adapter in the same manner, but slightly smaller overall.

7. When the entire arrangement is complete, glue one small floribunda to the hand of one of the models and a sprig of rice flower to the head of another.

8. Place the figures in happy, dancing positions and group them together with the two arrangements for a perfect performance.

TALL FRENCH TOLE VASE

8 stems of oncidium orchids
6 stems of Rothschild lilies
Eucalyptus
Floral foam
Moss

1. Fill the container with preservative-soaked floral foam and cover the top of the foam with moss. Work carefully because these flowers have very slender stems with little or no foliage to cover the mechanics.

2. Place the tallest orchid in the center and toward the back of the container. Fan the rest of the orchids out and to the sides, angled downward. Cut one or two stems short and place them toward the front.

3. Add the longest Rothschild lily, a bit shorter than the main orchid and out to the right. Continue to add the lilies to the front of the arrangement, scaling down the shape while filling in any voids.

4. Soften the edges with pieces of eucalyptus.

The 1983 Williamsburg Summit centerpieces were exquisitely arranged
in reproduction Chinese export bowls with a simple, loose construction
of peonies, ixia, freesia, nerines, and Queen Anne's lace.

Historic how-to

WILLIAMSBURG SUMMIT

Large decorated porcelain bowl

Red and pink peonies

Rose ixia

Queen Anne's lace

Freesia

Hot pink nerines

Floral foam

Moss

1. Fill a bowl with floral foam and moss and cover the edges with more moss.

2. Begin by placing the peonies in the bowl, since they are the largest and most prominent flowers.

3. Continue adding these rather evenly throughout the bowl to establish the overall size and rather round shape.

4. Fill in with freesia, nerines, and Queen Anne's lace.

5. Then finally add the ixia, keeping both the ixia and nerines shooting out of the arrangement.

bibliography

Aikman, Lonelle. *The Living White House* (Washington, D.C.: National Geographic Society, 1966).

Anthony, Carl Sferrazza. *America's First Families* (New York: Touchstone, 2000).

Baldrige, Letitia. *In the Kennedy Style* (New York: Doubleday, 1998).

Carter, Rosalynn. *First Lady from Plains* (Boston: Houghton Mifflin, 1984).

Clinton, Hillary Rodham. *An Invitation to the White House* (New York: Simon & Schuster, 2000).

Cross, Wilbur, and Ann Novotny. *White House Weddings* (New York: David McKay Co. 1967).

Ford, Betty. *The Times of My Life* (New York: Harper & Row, 1978).

Haller, Henry, and Virginia Aronson. *The White House Family Cookbook* (New York: Random House, 1987).

Johnson, Lady Bird. *A White House Diary* (New York: Holt, Rinehart and Winston, 1970).

Klapthor, Margaret Brown. *Official White House China* (Washington, D.C.: Smithsonian Institution Press, 1975).

Menendez, Albert J. *Christmas in the White House* (Philadelphia: Westminster Press, 1983).

Monkman, Betty C. *The White House: Its Historic Furnishings and First Families* (Washington, D.C.: White House Historical Association and Abbeville Press, 2000).

Montgomery, Ruth Shick. *Flowers at the White House: An Informal Tour of the Home of the Presidents of the United States* (New York: M. Barrows, distributed by W. Morrow, 1967).

Nixon, Julie. *Pat Nixon: The Untold Story* (New York: Simon & Schuster, 1986).

Seale, William. *The President's House* (Washington, D.C.: White House Historical Association, 1986).

Smith, Marie, and Louise Durbin. *White House Brides.* (Washington, D.C.: Acropolis Books, 1966).

Spillman, Jane Shadel. *White House Glassware: Two Centuries of Presidential Entertaining* (Washington, D.C.: White House Historical Association, 1989).

index

(Page numbers in *italics* refer to illustrations.)

art credits